REAL-TIME
PERSONAL COMPUTING

REAL-TIME PERSONAL COMPUTING

For Data Acquisition and Control

BABU JOSEPH

Associate Professor
Washington University, St. Louis

PRENTICE HALL, Englewood Cliffs, New Jersey 07632

Library of Congress Cataloging-in-Publication Data

Joseph, Babu
  Real-time personal computing.

  Bibliography: p.
  Includes index.
  1. Real-time data processing. 2. Microcomputers.
I. Title.
QA76.54.J67 1989   004'.33   88-17984
ISBN 0-13-767120-2

Editorial/production supervision and
  interior design: The Book Company
Cover design: Ben Santora
Manufacturing buyer: Mary Ann Gloriande

Trademark Acknowledgments

Apple II Macintosh	Apple Computer, Inc. 20525 Mariani Ave. Cupertino, CA 95014
Atari ST	Atari Corp. 1196 Borregas Ave. Sunnyvale, CA 94088
Amiga PET Commodore 64	Commodore Business Machines, Inc. 1200 Wilson Dr. Westchester, PA 19380
PC-DOS IBM IBM-PC IBM-AT PS/2	International Business Machines Corporation P.O. Box 1328 Boca Raton, FL 33432
CP/M CP/M-86	Digital Research, Inc. P.O. Box 579 160 Central Ave. Pacific Grove, CA 93950
TRS-80	Tandy Corporation 3209 Fondren Rd. Houston, TX 77063

 © 1989 by Prentice-Hall, Inc.
A Division of Simon & Schuster
Englewood Cliffs, New Jersey 07632

Printed in the United States of America
10 9 8 7 6 5 4 3 2 1

ISBN 0-13-767120-2

Prentice-Hall International (UK) Limited, *London*
Prentice-Hall of Australia Pty. Limited, *Sydney*
Prentice-Hall Canada Inc., *Toronto*
Prentice-Hall Hispanoamericana, S.A., *Mexico*
Prentice-Hall of India Private Limited, *New Delhi*
Prentice-Hall of Japan, Inc., *Tokyo*
Simon & Schuster Asia Pte. Ltd., *Singapore*
Editora Prentice-Hall do Brasil, Ltda., *Rio de Janeiro*

To my parents, Thomas Joseph Kunnemkote and Rosamma Joseph

Contents

Preface

The personal computer is revolutionizing our lives, both at home and at work. For many people in the technical community, the computer has become an integral part of their work. Personal computer systems are proving to be valuable productivity tools because of their low cost, versatility, word processing and graphics capability, and the large number of software tools available in the market. This book is intended as an introductory text for those who are interested in using the computer in a "real-time environment," that is, one in which the computer is connected to sensors, actuators, and control devices. Such applications are usually found in the laboratory, pilot plants, and production environments.

I have assumed that readers have some familiarity with computers and computer programming, perhaps through a first course in computing. But the required knowledge is minimal, and it is possible to design and build a computerized data acquisition and control (DAC) system without doing any program coding, thanks to advances in computer technology. What I have attempted to do is to provide a description of the technology involved with connecting the computer to the "real world" of sensors, switches, and instruments, so that you can make intelligent choices regarding the hardware and software required.

The book is organized according to the distinct features of a computerized DAC system. The first chapter is an overview of DAC systems; I recommend that you read this first, and then you can selectively read the remaining chapters of interest. Numerous examples are provided to illustrate and clarify the concepts. Questions are provided at the end of each chapter to review and check your understanding of the material that has been presented.

It is recommended that readers go through the book rather quickly at first to get an overview of the subject area. They can then concentrate on those areas of most interest to them. Since I have written this book for people with little or no prior background in the use of computers for data acquisition and control, I have kept the discussion at an elementary level at first. Details are added later in a step-by-step manner. The evolutionary nature of the field would have made any examples using actual hardware and software obsolete by the time the book is published. Hence the emphasis has been on generally applicable principles rather than specific application examples. The latter can be obtained from vendors of DAC software and hardware. Many manufacturers realize this need and provide good literature of the subject generally free for the asking.

A number of people deserve thanks for making this book possible. They include Dr. R. L. Motard for providing a sabbatical leave to complete the book, Dr. Y. M. Chan for some very interesting lectures on DAC systems, Dr. M. Dudukovic for his kind and encouraging words, and Drs. R. Powell, P. Deshpande, S. Munjal, and P. Mills for providing many valuable suggestions for improving the manuscript.

Much of this book was written while I was on sabbatical leave at an obscure place called Nediasala, which is nestled deep in the heart of the Vindya Mountain Range in Southern India. I would like to thank my parents for providing me with a peaceful place to think and formulate the majority of the chapters in the book. Finally, I would like to thank my wife for her patience and understanding while I was away completing this work.

REAL-TIME
PERSONAL COMPUTING

1

Introduction to Data Acquisition and Control Using Computers

This book is concerned with the use of personal computers for acquiring data and control of operations in a laboratory, pilot plant, or small-scale production facility. The primary objective is to familiarize the reader with this relatively new technology and to provide an introduction to various facets of this expanding field.

The term *microcomputer* is used here to refer to the desktop personal computers such as the IBM PC, Apple II, Macintosh, Commodore Amiga, TRS-80, Atari ST, and so on. The computing power of desktop computers has been steadily increasing while the cost has decreased. Today large-scale integration of microelectronic circuits has resulted in microcomputers that are the equivalent of yesterday's minicomputers. Besides, the mass marketing of microcomputer systems has resulted in greatly reduced costs of production. A wide variety of user-friendly software makes these desktop systems easy to use and adapt.

Microcomputers were popularized first for hobby and recreation but soon were established as a powerful tool in the workplace as well. Today, microcomputers are replacing computer terminals in the form of versatile workstations.

Gradually they have found a niche in the laboratory environment as well. Many instrument manufacturers are incorporating microprocessors into their equipment to provide greater intelligence and facility for communicating with other computers. An increasing number of manufacturers are furnishing the hardware and software necessary to interface microcomputers with the real world. The motivation for computerizing data acquisition and control comes from increased productivity. The microcomputer provides greater flexibility in how the data is acquired, processed, and reported.

Figure 1.1 depicts the scenario of this particular application of the microcomputer. The major components of a microcomputer-based *data acquisition and control system* (*DAC system*) are the microcomputer system itself; the sensors, actuators, and related

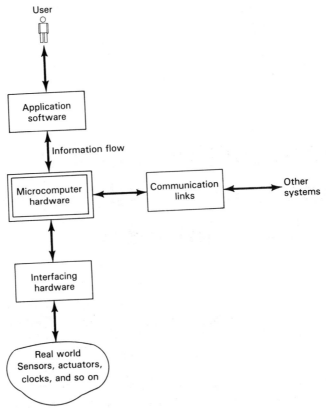

Figure 1.1 Elements of a computer-based data acquisition and control system

instrumentation that provide a connection with the "real world"; the interfacing hardware between the computer and the instrumentation; the software (program) that drives the microcomputer hardware; and the communication link with other computer systems. To design, purchase, and operate a DAC system, it is necessary to have a good understanding of each of these components. Providing this information is the intent of this book.

1.1 REAL-TIME COMPUTING

The topic of microcomputer-based DAC systems can be thought of as a subset of the field of real-time computing that is used to describe computing applications tied to time-dependent external events. Examples of real-time computing include

control of an aircraft in flight

an airline reservation system

an air-traffic monitoring system

computer control of a manufacturing unit

data acquisition from a pilot plant unit

Real-time computing is distinguished from other types of computing by the following features:

1. The computer must respond to external events.
2. The calculations must be performed with reference to the actual time of day.

The need to respond to external events makes the design, implementation, and testing of real-time systems far more difficult and complex. Such systems call for increased reliability and error-free execution of programs, since failures can be costly (computer or program failure can lead to failure of the external system or process that is being controlled by the computer).

1.2 A HISTORICAL PERSPECTIVE

The very first uses of real-time computing were in military applications related to missile firing and radar networks. The computers developed for this application were later adapted for industrial use. However, the growth of real-time applications was held back due to the high cost and need for alternative backup systems in case of computer failure.

The invention of the *minicomputer* was a major breakthrough in terms of the cost of building real-time systems. Computers such as Digital Equipment Corporation's PDP series of minicomputers found widespread application as a data acquisition and control device in the laboratory. The 1960s and 1970s can be regarded as the era of minicomputers in this field.

Another major breakthrough came with the arrival of the *microprocessor*. The most important feature these microprocessor-based systems brought to real-time computing was the ability to *distribute* the computing among many processors, thus increasing the reliability of such systems. The use of large-scale integration (the ability to put a large number of electronic circuits on small silicon wafers) led to decreasing costs.

One of the *microcomputers* (a computer based on a microprocessor) that found widespread application in the laboratory was the Apple II computer. This can be attributed to its low cost (from mass marketing), ease of use, and open architecture. The latter allowed easy interfacing of external (peripheral) devices to the computer. Soon after the introduction of the Apple II computer, a number of companies began to manufacture and market interface boards that allowed easy connection between the data acquisition and control signals and the computer. User-friendly software was also available. The major drawback of the Apple II was the limited capability of its microprocessor.

With the introduction of the IBM PC, microcomputers became as powerful as the minicomputers of the past. Again, the open architecture of this system made it a very popular candidate for use in DAC applications. Today, there are a large number of companies that manufacture and market DAC hardware and software for the IBM PC family of computers and compatibles.

Other microcomputers that have found applications in DAC systems include the DEC LSI-11 (which is also sold packaged as the MINC system), Commodore PET, and Radio Shack TRS-80. As newer microcomputers are introduced, these can be expected to find their way into the DAC area as well.

Because of this wide diversity in the field of microcomputers, the choices available to a person wishing to set up a DAC system are many. However, the basic principles involved are independent of the microcomputer used. In this book, we will concentrate on these principles, with examples that make reference to some specific models of microcomputers.

1.3 APPLICATION AREAS

Table 1.1 lists a number of application areas and possible functions of DAC systems. Some examples include the following.

Example 1   Data Logging

A weather station wants to monitor and record the variations in air temperature, humidity, wind speed, and wind direction. At the end of every 24 hours a report summarizing the variations, including the maximum and minimum of each variable, and a plot of the variations versus time is desired.

Example 2   Data Management

ABC Inc. is a small analytical laboratory. Each day, new batches of samples arrive for specific types of analysis with differing priorities. It is desired to automate the sample handling, scheduling of analytical instruments and technicians, status monitoring, and reporting of the results.

TABLE 1.1 APPLICATIONS OF
MICROCOMPUTER-BASED DAC SYSTEMS

Application areas	DAC functions
Laboratory instrumentation	Data logging
Testing equipment	Data analysis
Pilot plants	Data management
Experimental setups	Report generation
Small-scale production	Automatic control
User interfaces	Process optimization
	Process scheduling

Example 3   Data Communication

XYZ Oil Co. has a set of geographically distributed oil wells. Every day, production data from each well must be gathered and monitored. Production among the wells must be coordinated to satisfy the changing demand. Currently this is accomplished by telephone calls to various field operators. It is desirable to automate this process to increase accuracy and to provide more frequent updating.

Example 4   Manufacturing Automation

A machine tool manufacturing firm is interested in automating a portion of its operation that deals with the drilling of precisely positioned holes on a metal sheet. It is desirable to minimize loss of material and labor by having the drill positioned by computer control. The pattern of holes to be drilled is to be input into the computer.

Example 5   Laboratory Automation

An undergraduate laboratory exercise requires numerous titrations. It is desirable to build an automatic titration system that will determine the acidity of a given sample. The computer should inject acid or base into the solution to be titrated while monitoring the pH. At the end of each titration a brief report summarizing the run is to be provided to the student.

Example 6   Process Monitoring and Alarm

Company XYZ has a batch process for making a drug. The process lasts 24 hours and the temperature and the acidity in the reaction vessel must be constantly monitored. The process must be shut down in a safe manner if the cooling water supply is lost.

Each of the above examples requires a careful analysis before a suitable DAC system can be designed and built. After reading this book, you should be able to decide what questions to ask and how to select the appropriate tools necessary to build and install the DAC system.

1.4 OUTLINE OF THE BOOK

Figure 1.2 shows a road map of the book using an expanded version of Figure 1.1. A brief description of each chapter follows.

Chapter 2 gives an overview of DAC systems. This is a detailed discussion of each of the components that make up these systems.

Chapter 3 focuses on the aspects of the microcomputer system that are relevant to DAC systems. This chapter also develops and explains some of the common terms used in this field.

Chapters 4 and 5 discuss the hardware used in interfacing real-world sensors and actuators to the microcomputer. These chapters provide the background needed to design and select appropriate DAC peripherals. *Chapter 6* is a companion chapter that focuses on the sensing and signal conditioning aspects. Some general rules for connecting sensors and possible pitfalls to avoid are covered in this chapter.

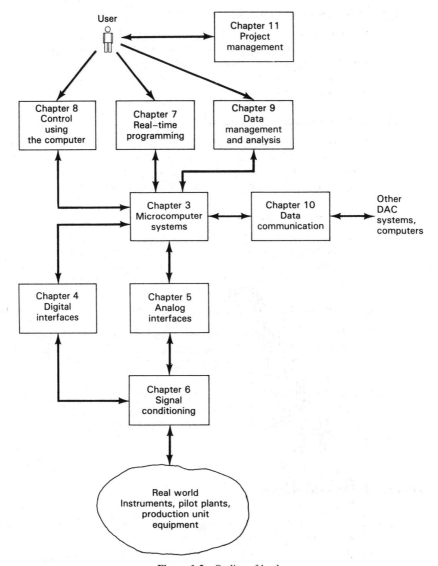

Figure 1.2 Outline of book

Chapters 7, 8, and 9 are concerned with software aspects of DAC systems. Chapter 7 focuses on specific software needs and types of software available for DAC users. Chapter 8 goes into some detail on the control theory and how to program the computer to accomplish feedback control of a process. Chapter 9 deals with the data analysis and data management functions of DAC systems.

Chapter 10 discusses the important area of data communications. Since many instruments are equipped today with microprocessors and because of the need to share data among many users, it is important to be able to set up communication networks that permit data transfer to and from the microcomputer.

Finally, in *Chapter 11,* the book concludes with some general discussion on the project management aspects of designing, building, and operating a DAC system.

SUMMARY

This chapter introduced the microcomputer-based data acquisition and control system. The major components of a DAC system were identified. (All of these components are discussed in greater detail in the following chapters.) Last, a number of application areas for microcomputer-based systems were identified, with examples.

REVIEW QUESTIONS

1. What are the components of a microcomputer-based DAC system?
2. What are some possible areas of automation within your organization? Can this be accomplished with a microcomputer-based DAC system?
3. Identify some possible benefits of computerized DAC systems.

2

Elements of Microcomputer-Based Data Acquisition and Control Systems

This is an overview chapter. It is intended to provide a general description of the functions and components of DAC systems. For the novice, it furnishes a summary of the possible uses of DAC systems. For an experienced user the chapter will be helpful in identifying new ways in which the microcomputer may be used in DAC applications.

2.1 TYPES OF DAC SYSTEMS

Data acquisition and control systems can be categorized according to the complexity of the computer system used. The lowest-cost DAC systems are built using component chips, but this is generally very time consuming and requires an understanding of digital electronic circuits. Since this is beyond the scope of this book, we will not consider such systems.

Single-Board DAC Systems

A single-board computer system consists of a printed circuit board containing a microprocessor, some memory, and interface chips. Such systems come with built-in software and a communication link to accept commands from a remote computer. Provisions for connecting (interfacing) process input and output signals are also provided.

Such systems are suitable for small applications requiring fewer than a dozen sensors with little or no analysis of the data. The μ-MAC 4000 systems manufactured by Analog Devices provide an example of such systems. Many of these systems require assembly language programming and hence are not suitable for people unfamiliar with computers. Their chief advantage is the low cost; also, they may be useful when the host computer system receiving the data must be placed far from the data source.

8-Bit Computer Systems

DAC systems built around computers such as the Apple II, TRS-80, and Commodore 64 belong to this category. These systems offer the advantages of low cost and ease of use. Due to the popularity of these computers for personal and home use, an extensive software library is available. Also, a variety of hardware interface boards for data acquisition and control are available from third-party vendors. This hardware and software greatly reduces the effort required to build a DAC system using these computers.

These systems can be used in applications involving 8–16 sensors, with fairly slow data collection rates. A minimal amount of data processing is achievable using this system. The main limitation of these systems is with the maximum memory capacity of the computer.

16-Bit Microcomputer Systems

The next level of sophistication is found in DAC systems built around 16-bit microcomputers such as the IBM PC. Such systems currently dominate the professional market of microcomputer-based DAC systems. They offer sufficient power to monitor 10–100 sensors, high-speed data acquisition from a smaller number of sensors, a fair amount of data processing, and large storage capacity. They can be used to monitor and control experimental setups, analytical instruments, pilot plants, and small-scale production units. A wide variety of hardware interface boards and software is available for these systems.

32-Bit Computer Systems

Microcomputers such as IBM PS/2 Model 80, Apple Macintosh, Commodore Amiga, and Atari ST are built around 32-bit microprocessors and hence pack more power. Since these are rather new entries in the market, they do not have as many hardware peripherals and as much software available as the popular 16-bit computers.

Some minicomputers such as the DEC VAX-11 also use 32-bit processors, and are more powerful. These minicomputers can support multiple users and have been used as a host computer for smaller microcomputer-based DAC systems. They may be used for managing and analyzing the data acquired from the micro-based DAC systems.

2.2 FUNCTIONAL CAPABILITIES OF MICROCOMPUTER-BASED DAC SYSTEMS

It is useful to enumerate the various ways in which microcomputer-based DAC systems may be employed in a laboratory or production environment. An overview of the functional components of DAC systems was provided in Chapter 1. Here we expand on these to further define the role of DAC systems. The functions are listed below with a brief description of each.

1. Read data from sensors and transmitters.   This is the data acquisition function. Sensors and transmitters generate various types of signals in electrical, mechanical, or other forms that must be read and stored in the computer memory. Besides, these readings must be acquired at prespecified times or intervals.

2. Store data in permanent form.   Most computer memories are volatile in nature. Provisions must therefore be made to transcribe the acquired data to a permanent storage medium from where the data can be recalled at a future date.

3. Display the acquired data.   Monitoring the progress of the process or the experiment linked to the computer requires a mechanism for the operator to view the data as it is being acquired. This could be in the form of tables, graphs, bar charts, and so on. It may be desirable to provide multiple colors for different types of data to call the attention of the operator to abnormal operating conditions.

4. Reduce and analyze the data.   Data acquired from sensors must be converted to appropriate units, checked for errors, and otherwise transformed. Some data might require further analysis such as peak detection and integration to yield meaningful results. Noisy data must be filtered to reduce the noise component. The availability of the microcomputer makes it feasible for a fair amount of data analysis to be performed as the data is being acquired, thus allowing the operator to make proper selection of operating variables.

5. Communicate the data.   Data acquired at one station is likely to be needed at other locations. This requires the capability to transmit and receive data to and from other sources, which may be other microcomputers, a host minicomputer, or a mainframe. If the other computer is far away, then it may be necessary to set up the communication link via telephone.

6. Prepare reports.   Data acquired from the plant or the experiment ends up in some form or other in one or more reports (the data may be in tabular or graphical format). Thus it is desirable to be able to manipulate the data into a form suitable for a report and to insert it into appropriately formatted reports. Tools must be available to tabulate data, graph data, type and edit reports, and print reports.

7. Enter data into a database.   A database is an organized way of storing data. Frequently the need arises for data collected by the DAC system to be organized and stored in a database. This calls for some special capabilities related to database management.

8. Send signals to actuators and controllers.   This refers to the control function of the DAC system. The computer should be able to send signals out to the real world to achieve control. The decisions on what signals to send out are taken by the control program. Depending on the type of actuator used, different kinds of hardware interfacing may be required.

The functional capabilities listed above cover a wide spectrum of needs. The hardware and software used in the DAC system depend greatly on the specific needs of the applications. The next two sections discuss the variety of hardware and software components used in DAC systems.

2.3 HARDWARE COMPONENTS OF A DAC SYSTEM

Figure 2.1 shows the hardware components of a DAC system necessary to meet the functional requirements outlined in the previous section. Only those components specific to DAC functions are shown here. A detailed discussion of the hardware components of the computer is deferred until the next chapter.

Analog Interface

The term *analog* is used to refer to signals that vary continuously over a fixed range. Examples of analog signal sources include thermocouples, pressure transducers, pH meters, flow sensing devices, level transmitters, and so on. Analog signals are typically read using meters, and the accuracy is limited by the precision with which the needle on the meter can be read. Digital signals on the other hand are displayed in numeric form, and the accuracy is dependent on the number of digits used to represent the signal.

The analog interface consists of two components. The first component, the signal conditioning unit, amplifies the signal, filters out high-frequency noise, changes the level of the signal, and performs other transformations necessary to obtain an acceptable voltage or current signal. The second component, the analog-to-digital conversion unit (A/D converter), generates computer-compatible digital (binary) signals that can be read and stored in the memory of the computer.

When outputting signals to analog devices such as control valves and power control units, a digital-to-analog (D/A) converter is needed.

Digital Interface

Devices that generate signals that are already in digital form include on/off switches, counters, and digital display instruments. Some signal conditioning may be required here also to reduce the digital signals to levels compatible with the voltages used within the computer. The function of the digital interface is to present the digital signals to the computer when requested.

Similarly, to send signals to devices that operate in a binary mode (devices such as relays, indicator lights, alarms) a digital output interface is required. Normally the inputting and outputting of digital information is achieved using a single digital interface.

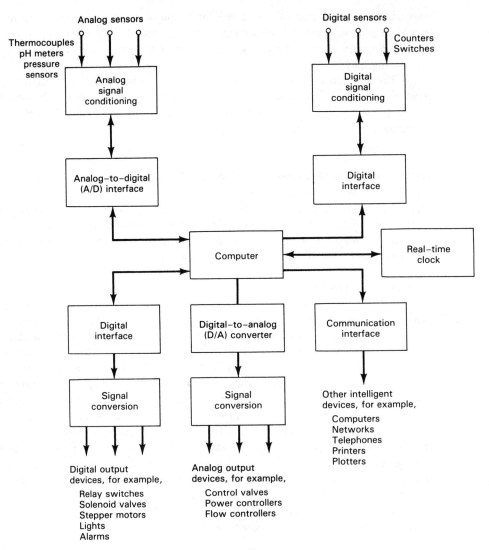

Figure 2.1 Hardware components of a DAC system

Communication Interface

The function of this hardware interface is to establish links with other computers, networks, the telephone line, and other intelligent instruments that have their own built-in microprocessors. The communication hardware will accept the data or commands to be sent and convert them to the appropriate signal to be transmitted over the communication link. There are a variety of modes in which this link can be established, and hence more than one communication hardware interface may be needed. Generally, links to printers, plotters, and similar computer peripheral devices are established using communication hardware interfaces.

Real-Time Clock

Although all computers come with a built-in clock, it is necessary to obtain a separate clock to keep track of the actual time of day. The clock is also set up with the capability to interrupt the computer at fixed frequency in order to facilitate execution of precisely timed real-time commands.

2.4 SOFTWARE COMPONENTS OF A DAC SYSTEM

The functional specifications of a DAC system outlined in Section 2.2 indicated the need for manipulating the data in a variety of ways after it has been acquired. This is facilitated by the software components of the DAC system, shown in Figure 2.2. The functions of these software components are discussed next.

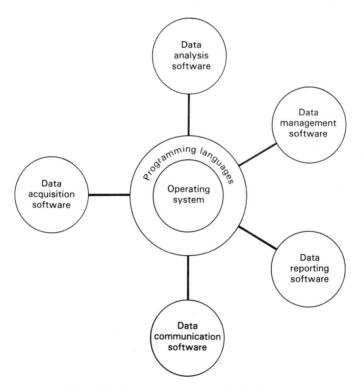

Figure 2.2 Software components of a DAC system

Data Acquisition Software

The acquisition of data using the hardware interface boards can be done at different levels of sophistication:

1. using machine language code
2. via calls from a higher-level language
3. through menu-driven software

The software required here is intimately tied to the hardware used. Most hardware manufacturers provide some software support either in the form of subroutine calls and/or as an integrated package. The former is flexible and adaptable whereas the latter is easier to set up and use. In general most DAC applications are unique and will require some customization.

Data Analysis Software

A fair amount of data analysis can be performed locally on the microcomputer used for acquiring the data. Some data conversion and checking can be done during the data acquisition stage and further analysis may be performed later. The latter include such complex transformations as linear and nonlinear regression (curve fitting), statistical analysis, data correlation, and Fourier transformation. These may be accomplished using a library of subroutines in a high-level language or using integrated data analysis software packages.

Information Management Software

The management of large volumes of data in a systematic way has typically been regarded as a problem in business data processing. Lately, it has been recognized that software tools developed to manage data can play a very important role in improving productivity in the laboratory as well. This has led to the development of special-purpose laboratory information management systems (LIMS). LIMS fall under the general category of database management systems.

Data Communication Software

Data communication between the microcomputer and other computers can be greatly facilitated by using these communication software packages. Most of these are menu-driven and allow exchange of data files over the communication line. If the link is to a network, then special network-driver software may be superimposed on the operating system of the computer. Using software, it is possible to make the microcomputer look like a terminal to a host mainframe or minicomputer (terminal emulation software).

2.5 ILLUSTRATIVE EXAMPLE

Consider the problem of automating a laboratory titration system. The titration is accomplished, as shown in Figure 2.3, by adding an acid to the solution at a slow rate until the solution is neutralized (pH = 7). The determination of the amount of acid to be added is complicated by the increase in the pH sensitivity of the solution as the neutralization point is approached.

It is desired to automate the titration process by means of an Apple II microcomputer.

Functional Requirements

Given a solution sample, acid must be added in precisely measured quantities while the pH is being constantly monitored. At the neutral point, the total amount of acid added must be computed and from this the concentration of the original sample solution can be calculated. A report summarizing the titration should be printed at the completion of the run.

Hardware Requirements

To read the pH of the solution in the beaker, a pH meter is used. To read the output of the pH meter, a signal amplifier and an A/D converter are required.

One approach to measuring the amount of acid added to the beaker is to use a metering pump. By turning the pump on for a specified time, a precisely measured

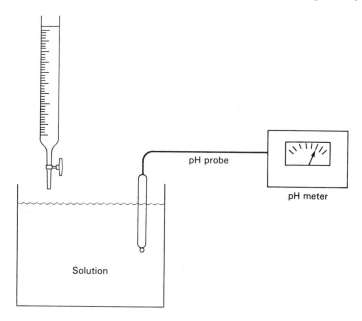

Figure 2.3 Titration experiment

quantity of acid can be delivered. To turn the pump on/off, a relay switch is required. The digital output from the computer can be used to turn the pump on/off. To keep track of the time duration a real-time clock is needed.

Software Requirements

The functional requirements of the software driver for the automatic titration are as follows:

1. At start of the run, enter the data regarding the sample (batch number, origin, date, and so on).
2. Driver subroutines are needed to read the pH and to output a value (on/off) to the relay switch.
3. During the run, the software should display the pH in the beaker, the total amount of acid added, and the computed concentration of original solution.
4. At the end of a titration, a report summarizing the results of the run should be printed.

The Complete DAC System

Figure 2.4 shows the complete DAC system. The output from the pH meter is amplified and read through the analog-to-digital converter. The relay is activated by sending a bit 0 or a bit 1 to the digital output device on the appropriate channel.

A calibration is required to correlate the amount of acid added as a function of the time duration for which the metering pump is turned on or off. The result is stored in the software that is used to drive the titration system.

The software requirements here are relatively modest and hence can be programmed in BASIC or another high-level language.

SUMMARY

This chapter gave an overview of the functional capabilities and the hardware and software needs of DAC systems. We identified a variety of areas in which the microcomputer can be suitably employed to improve productivity. Because of the unique nature of DAC systems, special interfacing hardware and software are needed. A variety of manufacturers provide this for popular microcomputer systems.

The software required in the DAC system also depends heavily on the application at hand. Some general-purpose software is available from hardware vendors and third-party software houses. The choices available and costs vary a great deal, and hence it is important to have a good understanding of the hardware and software requirements of the DAC application to make a judicious selection.

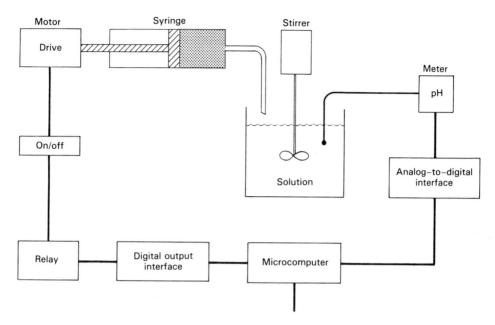

Figure 2.4 DAC system for automatic titration

REVIEW QUESTIONS

1. List the various ways in which a DAC system may be employed in a
   (a) laboratory environment
   (b) production environment
2. Consider the examples cited in Chapter 1. For each one try to develop
   (a) functional requirements
   (b) hardware requirements
   (c) software requirements
3. Develop a DAC system for patient monitoring in an intensive care unit of a hospital. What are the input requirements? What are possible output requirements? What type of information must be provided to the medical team?

REFERENCES

MELLICHAMP, D. A., ed. *Real-Time Computing with Applications to Data Acquisition and Control.* New York: Van Nostrand Reinhold, 1983.
This is a comprehensive book discussing all aspects of real-time computing. It is intended primarily for the minicomputer user. A rather good introductory book.

FOSTER, C. C. *Real-Time Programming: Neglected Topics.* Reading, MA: Addison-Wesley, 1982.

This book goes into some detail on the software aspects of real-time computing with some very good examples. It is recommended for people who want to get into some machine language–level programming.

CLINE, B. E. *Automated Data Acquisition*. New York: Petrocelli Books, 1983.

LISCOUSKI, J. G., ed. *Computers in the Laboratory*. ACS Symposium Series. Washington, DC: American Chemical Society, 1984.

This book contains a collection of papers discussing various issues in the use of computers in the laboratory. Some good tutorial papers are included.

ANNINO, R., and R. D. DRIVER. *Scientific and Engineering Applications with Personal Computers*. New York: Wiley Interscience, 1986.

3

Microcomputer Systems

3.1 INTRODUCTION

We will use the term *microcomputer* to refer to a computer system built around a micro-processor. The microcomputer is the central part of a DAC system. The technology of the microcomputer is relatively new, and a newcomer to the field is faced with a wide range of choices to make in setting up a system. The purpose of this chapter is to provide a basic understanding of the technology that is pertinent to a DAC system.

Bits, Bytes, and Words

All operations done by the computer are eventually reduced to manipulations of binary digits: 0 and 1. In computer jargon this is referred to as a *bit*. A group of 4 bits is referred to as a *nibble* and a group of 8 bits is called a *byte*. Most operations are carried out in groups of 8 bits, and hence the term byte arises frequently. For example, all the alphabetic characters and numerals (the alphanumerics) can be coded into 8 bits, as follows:

Symbol	Computer representation
A	00100001
B	00100010
C	00100011

With 8 bits, a total of 256 (2^8) different characters can be represented. Later on we will discuss some accepted standards for coding these characters. The above example used the ASCII (American Standard Code for Information Interchange) code.

A *word* refers to the number of bits that can be manipulated by the central processing unit of the computer. The word length in effect determines to a large extent the
capability of the computer. Computers with a word length of 8 bits are called 8-bit
computers, those with a word length of 16 bits are called 16-bit computers, and so on.
Examples of 8-bit computers include the Apple II, Commodore 64, and Z-80. Examples
of 16-bit computers include the IBM PC series, Compaq Portable, and Leading Edge. The
newest family of microcomputers uses 32-bit processors and includes the Apple Macintosh, IBM PS/2, Atari ST, Commodore Amiga, and Microvax II. Because of the additional capabilities of these 32-bit processors, they can be expected to dominate the market
in the future.

3.2 MICROCOMPUTER ARCHITECTURE

We will use the term *microcomputer* to mean a computer system consisting of a microprocessor; memory; input/output devices such as keyboard, video display, and printer;
permanent storage medium; communication interfaces; and associated software. Figure
3.1 shows the architecture of a typical microcomputer system.

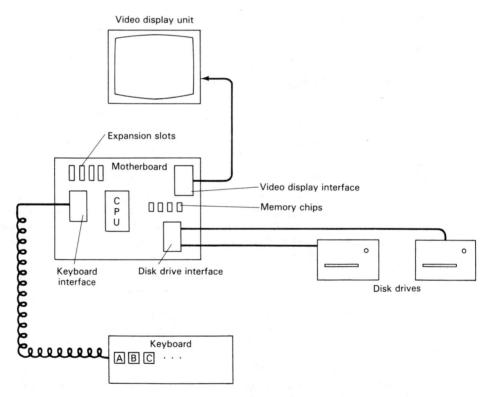

Figure 3.1 Physical layout of components of a microcomputer system

The heart of this system is the *microprocessor*—also called the *central processing unit* or *CPU*. The microprocessor is a rectangular-shaped integrated circuit (IC) chip with a number of pins attached to the bottom through which all the electrical connections are made.

The structure of these connections is shown in Figure 3.2. All the pins of the CPU together constitute the *CPU bus*. Physically the CPU bus can be regarded as a set of parallel wires, each of which carries 1 *bit* of information. Whether the bit is 1 or 0 is determined by the voltage level: Typically 0–1.5 V is regarded as a ''0'' and 3.5–5 V is regarded as a ''1.'' The bus is further divided into three segments:

Data bus: lines carrying data

Address bus: lines carrying source or destination address of data

Control bus: lines that determine when and how the data transaction takes place

Instructions to be executed by the CPU are stored in the *memory,* which consists of a set of storage locations, each with a unique address. The memory also retains the data on which the operations are performed. The CPU operates by retrieving instructions from memory one at a time and then executing these instructions. Thus memory serves a dual purpose: that of storing the instructions (or program) and also the data.

Every memory location is assigned a unique number called its *address*. When the CPU wants to store a data item in memory, it puts the address of the memory location,

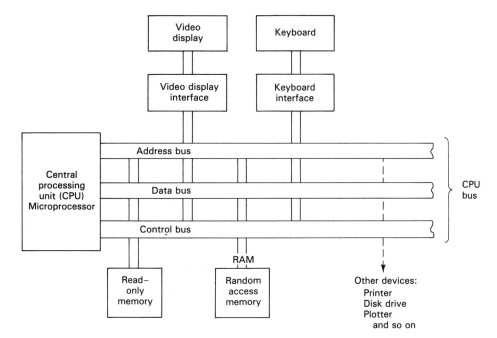

Figure 3.2   Microcomputer system architecture

expressed in binary form, on the address bus and the binary bits to be stored in the data bus. This is then followed by appropriate signals on the control lines, which allow the transfer of the data from the data bus to the memory location.

There are two ways that peripheral devices are linked with the CPU. For essential items such as memory and keyboard, the interface unit is built into the motherboard (see Figure 3.1). Others such as printers and plotters require special interface cards. Expansion slots are provided on the motherboard to plug in these interface boards. Not all microcomputers have this important feature. Having the slots makes it easier to expand the capabilities of the system by adding new peripherals.

An important aspect of a microcomputer system not shown in Figures 3.1 and 3.2 is *software;* that is, the programs and instructions that make these hardware units perform the desired tasks. The hardware components depicted in Figures 3.1 and 3.2 are discussed in more detail in the next section, and software components are covered in Section 3.4.

3.3 THE CENTRAL PROCESSING UNIT (CPU)

The CPU consists of millions of tiny electronic circuits built into a small silicon wafer. Functionally, the CPU can be divided into four segments, as shown in Figure 3.3.

> *A clock:*   This clock generates pulses at a fixed frequency. The speed at which the CPU executes instructions is determined by the frequency of this clock. Typically this clock rate is set at a

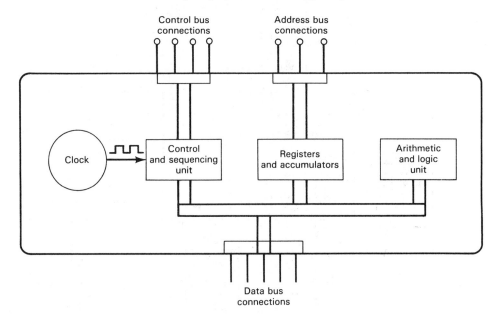

Figure 3.3   Structure of the central processing unit

few megahertz (10^6 cycles/sec). For example, the clock rate on an IBM PC is set at 4.77 MHz.

Accumulators and registers:	These are temporary locations for storing data on which the CPU is performing operations.
Control unit:	This unit determines the sequence of actions taken by the CPU.
Arithmetic and logic unit:	This unit performs operations such as addition, subtraction, comparison, and so on.

Complex arithmetic operations such as multiplication and division can be handled by a separate chip, called the *math coprocessor* (also known as the *arithmetic processor* and *floating point calculation chip*), which is an optional item with most microcomputers. Typically a space is provided on the motherboard to install this chip for the user who intends to do a lot of arithmetic processing with the system. Arithmetic operations such as multiplication and division may also be carried out in software, but at much slower rates.

The bus structure (and instruction set) used by each CPU is unique and is not interchangeable with other manufacturers. Some bus standards have been proposed in the past but none have taken hold. This aspect makes it difficult to interchange hardware among different computer systems.

Microprocessor chips are identified by numbers designated by the manufacturer. These are characterized by the word length (the maximum number of bits that can be manipulated by the CPU in one instruction). Typical word lengths are 8 bits, 16 bits, and 32 bits. The Apple II uses an 8-bit processor (6502 by Mostech), the IBM PC uses a 16-bit processor (8088 by Intel), and the Apple Macintosh uses a 32-bit processor (68000 by Motorola). Table 3.1 shows some popular microcomputer systems and the CPUs used therein.

TABLE 3.1   POPULAR MICROPROCESSORS AND MICROCOMPUTERS

Processor	Word size	Typical systems
Intel 8080	8-bit	
Zilog Z80	8-bit	Heath
		TRS-80 Model III
		Timex/Sinclair
		HP 125
Mostech 6502	8-bit	Commodore 64
		Apple II
Intel 8088	8-bit data/16-bit processor	IBM PC
		DEC Rainbow
		TI Professional
Intel 80286	16-bit data/16-bit processor	IBM PC/AT
Motorola 68000	32-bit	Apple Macintosh
		HP 200
		Commodore Amiga
		Atari 520ST

Input Devices

The primary input device of course is the *keyboard*. In addition to the usual typewriterlike alphabetic and numeric keys, the keyboard also contains special keys designed to enhance the number of characters that can be entered through the keyboard. The ALT and CTRL keys function in a similar manner to the shift key. Sometimes two keystrokes are used to designate one character. This is done in conjunction with the ESC key. There may also be a number of ''function'' keys whose use can be customized to the software being used.

A *mouse* is another input device that is popular with some systems. The mouse can be used to move the position of a cursor on a screen and is hence useful in selecting items from menus. By moving the mouse around on a flat surface, the location of the cursor on the screen can be changed. Some software purchased commercially is tailored to use mouse-driven inputs for convenience. Microsoft Word, a word processing program, is an example of such software. Having a mouse can be helpful in program development.

Another input device used in menu selection is the *touch sensitive screen,* which detects the location of the item pointed at by a finger on the screen. Other forms of input such as *spoken input* may also become readily available in the future as this technology develops.

A *digitizer* can be used to transfer drawings and figures from paper to screen.

Output Devices

The *cathode ray tube (CRT)* is a common medium of output from the computer. Other terms used for this device are *video display unit (VDU)* and *screen*. There are many varieties of video displays. They can be broadly categorized into *monochrome* or *color displays*.

Monochrome displays show only one color (green, blue, or amber are the common colors). Characters are formed on the screen by combining many dots. Typical screen size is 25 lines × 80 characters.

Color displays come in two types, *composite video* and *RGB (red, green, and blue)*. The former uses the same technology as regular television and has limited resolution. RGB monitors are more expensive but offer superior resolution. Color monitors are most useful in graphics. Graphics are obtained by dividing the screen into thousands of dots (called *pixels*) and then projecting the appropriate color on each pixel. Typical resolutions are 300 × 200 (low-resolution graphics), 600 × 500 (medium resolution), and 1000 × 1000 (high resolution). Medium or high resolution is required to obtain good character displays on a graphics screen. If one does mainly character displays, a monochrome display is preferable, because it offers better resolution for character displays than a low-resolution graphics display. For data acquisition and control purposes, a color monitor with at least medium-resolution capability is recommended, since many commercial software packages use this feature.

A second common output device is the *printer*. Printers come in basically three types: *dot matrix, impact,* and *laserjet*. Dot matrix printers produce characters by a combination of dots. They are generally priced lower than the other types and come with a range of speed and quality. The quality is determined by the number of dots used to make up a character and the speed of printing. Some dot matrix printers have a letter quality mode (slow speed) and a draft mode. Dot matrix printers are capable of producing a variety of character fonts and sizes. They are also capable of reproducing the graphics displays from the screen. It is possible to obtain dot matrix printers that can reproduce color graphics as well.

The second option you have is to obtain a letter quality impact printer, which prints by striking formed letters onto a ribbon. A common variety here is the daisy wheel printer. They are generally slower than dot matrix printers and cannot be used to reproduce graphics. The third option used by desktop publishers is to purchase a laserjet or inkjet printer; these operate on a principle similar to the one used in copiers. The characters are formed by combining dots but at a very high density. This high density gives the output produced on these devices the look and feel of commercial printing. They are also capable of reproducing graphics. The costs of these printers have come down significantly, and some are available for a few thousand dollars.

An alternative to producing hard copy graphics output is to use *plotters*. These generally give higher quality than dot matrix printers. One disadvantage of these devices is that they are slow. Multicolor plotters are available to reproduce color graphics. Again, for DAC applications, high-quality black and white graphs and charts can be reproduced on a laserjet printer.

Since printers are generally slow devices compared to the CPU, they are usually provided with some local memory for storing information to be printed. This way the CPU can send the information to this local memory and be available for other programs or tasks. The printer will then output the information from the local memory at its speed. It is also possible to set aside a portion of the computer's memory for this purpose. This is known as *printer spooling,* and the memory set aside for this purpose is called the *buffer memory.* This is a software function, and usually the software has to be purchased separately.

Memory

The term *memory* is used to designate storage within the computer that can be accessed (read from or written to) by the CPU at its clock rate. It is used for storing the program being executed as well as any data associated with the program. *ROM* stands for *read-only memory* and has the property that data and programs stored therein are not erased when power is turned off. ROM is used to store programs such as the start-up routines that need to be run every time power is turned on. Programs that never need to be changed are candidates for storage in ROM.

RAM (*random access memory*) on the other hand is volatile. The items stored there are destroyed when power is turned off. However, you can read as well as write on RAM memory. RAM comes in chips of 8K, 64K, and 256K bits.

In some computers, such as the Apple II, memory is limited to 64 kilobytes (Kb) due to addressing limitations. Note that each memory must have a unique address, and hence the maximum memory allowable in a computer is dependent on the size of the address bus on the CPU (the number of lines used for determining the address).

EPROMs (*erasable programmable read-only memory*) fall into a category of memory chips that can store data permanently but in erasable form using ultraviolet light. They require special equipment to erase and to write on. They are useful for storing programs that do not have to be changed often.

Permanent Storage Devices

Data and programs may be stored permanently in a number of ways. The common medium in use today is disk storage devices. These come in many types and capacities.

Flexible disks of size 5¼″ and 3½″ are in common use today. A 5¼″ diskette can store up to 360 Kb of information (double-sided, double-density type) or 1.2 Mb in the high-density mode. Early versions of this medium used single-sided and single-density disks, but these are no longer popular. Both the Macintosh and the IBM PS/2 use 3.5″ diskettes as the standard.

One disadvantage of these disk drives is the relatively slow speed of data transfer between the memory of the computer and the diskette. An alternative here is to use nonremovable disks, called *hard disks,* which are disks in a totally enclosed drive. They offer faster access speeds and larger storage capacities (10, 20, 40, and 60 Mb). Higher-capacity disk drives can be expected in the near future. A removable version of the hard disk is also now on the market.

Magnetic tape is another common permanent storage medium. The disadvantage here is with slow access times. Data must be read sequentially, and so it is not easy to use this device as an online storage retrieval device. Tapes come in reel types and cassette types. Reel tapes can store very large amounts of data (up to 100 Mb are feasible) and hence are a commonly used backup medium.

As with any storage medium, the data can be accidently erased, due to physical damage or software failure. Hence proper backup is essential. Backups are provided by making additional copies and storing these under protected conditions. Another alternative is to provide a tape drive as an integral part of the hard disk. Backup can then be accomplished more easily.

3.4 MICROCOMPUTER SOFTWARE

Software used in the operation of the computer system can be divided into three major categories: operating system, programming languages, and application programs.

Operating System

The function of the operating system software is to take care of the housekeeping tasks associated with the operation of the computer. When the computer is switched on, a program residing in ROM that is sometimes called the *basic input/output system* (*BIOS*) is run automatically. This may include some self-checking, such as testing the memory for possible defects, and so on. This program then loads the disk operating system from the system diskette into the RAM memory, where it resides until the power is turned off. This operating system will appear on the screen with a ready prompt. When this prompt appears, the computer will accept the operating system commands. Examples of operating system commands for the IBM PC-DOS are

Command	Response
DIR	Displays a directory of files on the disk.
PRINT MYFILE	Prints a file named *myfile*.
TYPE MYFILE	Displays contents of a file on the CRT.
FORMAT	Prepares a new disk for writing files.
COPY abc xyz	Copies file named *abc* onto a file named *xyz*.

Operating systems differ from one manufacturer to another. For the Apple II computer, an operating system called *Apple DOS* is used. *CP/M (control program/ microprocessor)* is another popular operating system for 8-bit microcomputers. Microcomputer systems built around the Z-80 and Intel 8080 microprocessors use this operating system.

For 16-bit microcomputers the most widely accepted operating system is *MS-DOS* by Microsoft Corporation. This operating system is called *PC-DOS* when sold for the IBM PC. The examples cited above are taken from this operating system. As the technology improves, newer versions of the operating system that are downward compatible—that is, that use the same instruction set as the previous version—are introduced. These are identified by the version number 1.0, 2.0, 2.1, and so on.

An important item to remember here is that software developed under one operating system may not be compatible with another operating system. Disks created under one operating system will not be readable under another. With new, more powerful computers, it will be possible to run more than one operating system. The newer operating systems incorporate the capability of running more than one program at any time and being able to view the progress of each one through different *windows* on the screen. The user can switch among the different programs. Such operating systems are called *multitask operating systems*. When used with DAC systems, multitasking has a different connotation, which we will discuss later.

Programming Languages

Almost all the programming languages used in larger computers are also available in microcomputers. These languages come in two types, *compiler languages* and *interpretive languages*.

Compiler languages first translate the program written by the user into machine code to create what is called an *object module,* which contains the machine language instructions equivalent to the original program. This is known as the *compilation phase*.

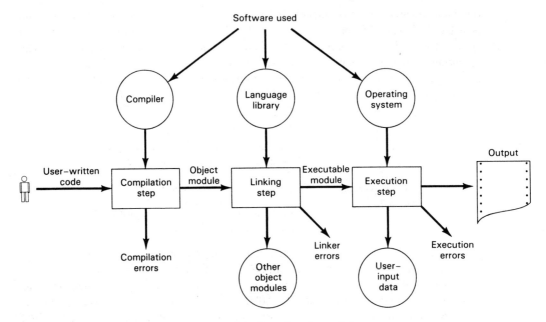

Figure 3.4 Execution of compiled programs

At the next phase, called the *linking phase,* this object module is taken and combined with other library modules to create an executable program called the *load module.* This module is then loaded into memory and is executed. The entire sequence of events is shown in Figure 3.4.

Interpretive languages use another approach to execute programs. First the entire language module that translates and executes the instructions written in the programming language is loaded into memory. A portion of the memory is reserved for the storage of the user's programs. In the execution phase each line of the user's program is read and successively translated and executed. Figure 3.5 shows the sequence of events during the execution of a program using interpretive languages.

Compiler languages offer greater efficiency, modularity, and speed. Interpreters on the other hand offer greater flexibility during the program development stage. Interpretive languages are best suited for short programs.

For microcomputers, *BASIC* is probably the most widely available language. It comes mostly in interpretive form, but compilers are also available. This language is easy to learn and fairly versatile. One of its nice features is its graphics capability.

FORTRAN is another language that is widely used in scientific and engineering computing. This language has some commonly accepted standards (FORTRAN-66, FORTRAN-77), which allows for easy portability of programs between machines and among operating systems. Many FORTRAN compilers offer extensions to the standard, but these

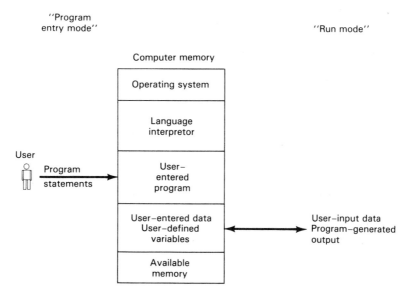

Figure 3.5 Structure of interpretive languages

features should be used with caution, since the portability will be impaired. FORTRAN compilers are available for most popular microcomputers.

PASCAL and *C* are two languages preferred by system programmers. The former is known for its structure and easy error checking capabilities. The latter is relatively new, but has taken a strong foothold among system developers because of its efficiency and versatility.

Application Software

The majority of users of microcomputers depend on special-purpose application software to accomplish their tasks. This software aids them in developing application packages for their specific needs.

The following kinds of application software should be of interest to users of DAC systems:

word processing software

spreadsheet software

database management software

software specifically built for DAC systems

Some very powerful *word processing* packages are now available at low cost. The choice is limited when it comes to displaying special characters (such as Greek letters or mathematical symbols) on the screen. Some word processors can print special characters but cannot display them on the screen. Word processing software can also double as an editor for writing programs and correcting errors in a program, and also in entering and editing data stored in a file. Every system should have a word processing program, but do not spend a lot of money on this software unless you plan to use the computer a great deal for preparing reports and other documents. Compatibility of the files generated with other word processing facilities used in your office environment should also be considered when selecting a word processing package.

Spreadsheet software refers to programs that allow tabular calculations to be performed with ease. They are very popular in accounting and business, where a great many calculations are done in tabular format. Spreadsheets also have uses in science and engineering. Some spreadsheet programs such as Lotus 1-2-3 are very powerful, incorporating graphics and data management facilities in addition to number crunching. These additional features can be used to advantage in the storage and processing of data in a laboratory.

Database management software (DBMS) incorporates the ability to store, retrieve, and manipulate large amounts of data on a computer without having to worry about how the data is physically stored in the storage device. Data manipulation such as sorting, retrieving of data that satisfy certain criteria, creating new tables from existing files, and adding password protection can be achieved using simple commands to the DBMS system. Again, a large number of companies are offering products in this area, and having access to such software is highly recommended if you are dealing with large volumes of data.

Special-purpose software for data acquisition and control can be classified into the following categories:

integrated systems

software for specific applications

software for specific interface hardware in the form of subroutines callable from a high-level language such as BASIC or FORTRAN

Integrated systems combine the data collection, data display, control functions, data storage and data analysis, and so on in one package. The user generally works with menu-driven commands. Such packages are available for laboratory applications (which concentrate on data analysis) and for control applications (with an emphasis on real-time display and monitoring). Software for specific applications such as gas chromatography analysis, fast Fourier transform, curve fitting, and scientific plotting is also available.

DAC software requirements and availability are discussed in more detail in Chapters 7, 8, and 9.

SUMMARY

A microcomputer system consists of a microprocessor interfaced with devices for storing data (memory, disk drives), inputting data (keyboard, mouse, touchscreen), and outputting data (screen, printer, plotter, telephone), and the software that makes all these components work in an integrated fashion. Microprocessors are classified according to their word length, which signifies the maximum number of bits they can manipulate. We started with 8-bit microprocessors, migrated to 16-bit chips, and currently 32-bit microprocessor-based systems are appearing on the market. Each level improves the capabilities of the system by an order of magnitude.

An important element that links the various components of the microcomputer system is the CPU bus. Each microprocessor has a unique bus structure. Another distinguishing feature is the basic sets of machine-coded instructions that the microprocessor is designed for. These two differences make it virtually impossible to transport or interchange hardware and software among different systems. The only standards that exist are for higher-level languages, but even here the standards are rather weakly enforced by systems.

Thus a new user shopping for a microcomputer system is well advised to consider fully all the hardware and software requirements before making a decision. Once the basic system is selected, further choices are narrowed down considerably because of compatibility requirements. The possibility of expanding and upgrading the system to accommodate future growth should also be kept in mind when selecting the microcomputer system configuration.

REVIEW QUESTIONS

1. What is the function of the CPU bus? What are the three components of this bus?
2. What is a motherboard of a microcomputer? What is meant by expansion slots?
3. What are the different types of memory that can be used with a microcomputer? What is meant by volatile memory?
4. Explain qualitatively how the CPU transfers data from memory to a peripheral device such as the printer.
5. What are the functions of the operating system?
6. What is the difference between compiler languages and interpretive languages?
7. Cite examples of commercially available application packages for
   (a) database management
   (b) spreadsheet analysis
   (c) word processing
   (d) communications
   Evaluate the capabilities of a few selected packages using vendor-supplied information.
8. List the various components of a microcomputer system, their functions, and approximate costs. What would be critical items in data acquisition systems?

REFERENCES

There has been a considerable increase in the literature available on microcomputer systems in the last few years. Most bookstores now have a large selection of books and magazines devoted to computers. Some introductory books are

RODWELL, P. *The Personal Computer Handbook*. New York: Barron's, 1983.

DREVNICKS, D. F., ED. *IBM Personal Computer Handbook*. Berkeley, CA: And/Or Press, 1983.

FLORES, J., AND C. TERRY. *Microcomputer Systems,* New York: Van Nostrand Reinhold, 1982.

DOLOGITE, D. G. *Using Small Business Computers*. Englewood Cliffs, NJ: Prentice-Hall, 1984.

4

Interfacing Digital Signals

4.1 INTRODUCTION

In this chapter we consider the hardware and software interface for inputting and outputting digital signals to and from the real world. By digital we mean signals that have a binary state: on/off, high/low, 0 V/5 V, up/down, and so on. Digital *input* signals refer to those signals that are read by the computer. Digital *output* signals refer to signals that are sent out by the computer. Examples of digital input signals are

operator-activated switches
switches activated by the process
signals from digital thermometers
signals from frequency counters
signals sent from a remote computer

Examples of digital output signals are

lights turned on/off by computer
solenoid valves
alarms activated by computer
signals sent to a remote computer/printer
a pump turned on/off by computer
a heater turned on/off by computer

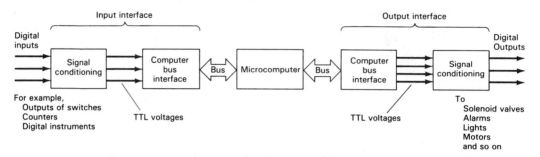

Figure 4.1   Interfacing of digital input/output signals

In this chapter we will focus our attention on digital interfaces other than those used in communication between intelligent devices such as between computers or between the computer and a printer. The latter is covered in Chapter 10.

Interfacing digital signals is simplified by the fact that all information is stored in the computer's memory in digital form. In practice it is complicated by the fact that the computer is a very fast machine, whereas most real devices are slow by comparison. Also, the signal levels of digital information used inside the computer may differ from the requirements of the signal in the real world. These facts require that the interfacing of digital signals be done in a two-step process, as shown in Figure 4.1.

The first step involves converting the binary or digital signals to levels compatible with the signals used within the computer. This is the function of the signal conditioning unit. The second step involves transferring the data in and out of the computer's bus. These steps are discussed in the next two sections.

4.2 DIGITAL INTERFACE HARDWARE

A brief description of the principles involved in transferring data to and from the computer's bus is given here. As indicated in the previous chapter, the bus is divided into three segments:

> data bus
>
> address bus
>
> control bus

For an 8-bit computer, such as the Apple II, the data bus is 8 bits wide and the address bus is 16 bits wide. The 16 bits of the address bus can be used to designate $2^{16} = 65,136$ different addresses, ranging from

$$0 \quad 000 \quad 000 \quad 000 \quad 000 \quad 000$$

to

$$1 \quad 111 \quad 111 \quad 111 \quad 111 \quad 111$$

Most addresses are used for the memory of the computer, and a few are reserved for external input/output devices including digital interfaces. *Every device* connected to the bus must have a *unique address* associated with it. When the computer wishes to output a signal to this device, it first puts the address of this device on the address bus. An address decoder on the device alerts the device to receive the data. Next the computer transfers the data to be output from memory to the data bus. A full byte is transferred at any one time. After the data is put on the data bus, a timing signal is sent on the control bus that alerts the device that the data is ready to be read. The device should capture the data before the next clock cycle on the CPU. Since the clock rate of the CPU is of the order of a few megahertz, the data must be captured by the device in a fraction of a microsecond. This is accomplished using some chips called *latches,* which pick up the digital output signal from the data bus and hold it temporarily. All 8 bits are transferred to the device simultaneously.

Similarly, when the computer wants to read a byte from an input device, it first puts the address of the device on the address bus and then sends a signal to indicate that it is ready to accept the data on the data bus. At this point, the device must place the data on the data bus momentarily and then give up control of the data bus. Again the data transfer takes place in one clock cycle of the microprocessor.

Note that in both cases, inputting and outputting, the CPU is in command. Since the CPU is merely executing program instructions, ultimate control of the sequence of events rests with the programmer or the user. The instructions can be coded in machine language or some higher-level language such as BASIC or FORTRAN. Later on in this chapter we will discuss examples of how this is accomplished.

Note that a full 8 bits of data are transferred in the case of an 8-bit computer. Sometimes it may be desirable to transfer only 1 bit. It is possible to set up the device to receive only a limited number of bits.

Interrupt Inputs

Interrupts are another form of digital input, but they operate in a totally different manner. As mentioned earlier, digital inputs are read by software instructions. There may arise instances where we would like an external event (for example, the closing of a switch) to trigger some program in memory. This is the purpose of the interrupt lines. Normally, when an interrupt is activated, the CPU temporarily suspends execution of the current program and jumps to a preset location in memory.

The handling of interrupts is made easier through the use of real-time operating systems (RTOS). More detail regarding interrupt handling is given in Chapter 7.

4.3 DIGITAL SIGNAL CONDITIONING

Almost all computers operate using signals that are TTL (transistor-transistor logic) compatible with 0–1.5 V signals treated as logic 0 and 3.5–5 V signals treated as logic 1 (there are a few exceptions to this rule where the reverse logic is used). Signals that are in between are indeterminate and can lead to unpredictable results. Thus the digital signal lines to be read by the computer must be reduced to this level by the signal conditioning unit.

The need for signal conditioning arises more frequently with output signals. The TTL signal available from the computer has very little power (usually 1–2 mA current can be drawn). This is sufficient only to power an LED (light emitting diode). Greater strength is achieved by using relay switches. The use of relays is illustrated in Figure 4.2. The relay will open or close depending on whether the input signal is 0 or 5 V. A relay can be used to turn a light bulb (requiring 110 V supply) on or off depending on whether the output to the channel is 0 or 1.

In cases where high voltages are involved as in the preceding example, it is desirable to provide protection for the low-voltage circuit by isolating it from the high-voltage line. This is accomplished by using optically activated transistors and thus avoiding any direct metal contacts between the two lines. This minimizes the possibility of damage to the computer by occasional spikes in the high-voltage line.

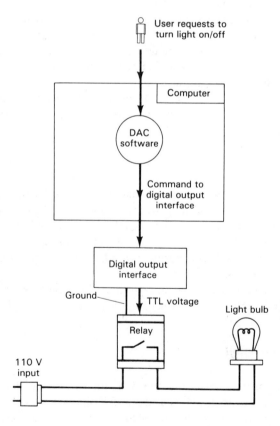

Figure 4.2 Illustrating the use of a relay switch to turn a light bulb on/off with the aid of a computer

4.4 COMMERCIAL DIGITAL INPUT/OUTPUT SYSTEMS

Digital input/output interface boards for microcomputers come in two types:

1. Interface boards that plug into the expansion slots on the motherboard.
2. Interface boards that plug into a separate chassis or box external to the computer. This expansion box is then linked to the computer's CPU by using a ribbon cable and a card that plugs into the expansion slot.

Some manufacturers combine the digital input/output functions with other interfaces, such as a real-time clock and/or analog interface devices. This is because of the relative simplicity of the digital interface circuitry. Prices range from a few hundred dollars to a thousand dollars or more.

The choice of the interface board used depends on the following criteria:

1. The total number of digital input and digital output channels needed.
2. Signal levels needed for the digital I/O. Some manufacturers offer switch selectable output ranges.
3. The availability of signal conditioning circuitry. If this uses high voltages (110 V or more), then the signal conditioning should include optical isolation and should be kept outside the computer's chassis. You do not want to risk bringing in high-voltage lines inside the computer box.
4. The availability of software to facilitate input and output. This software may be in the form of subroutine calls from BASIC, FORTRAN, and so on, or in the form of integrated software. The former give greater flexibility, but the latter may be more convenient to use.

It would be preferable if the software can address each digital input channel separately rather than all channels at once. In the latter case, the user will have to decode a byte to see what each bit is. A partial list of manufacturers that make interface boards for popular microcomputer systems is given at the end of Chapter 5.

Example 1   Temperature Alarm

The temperature of a stirred tank reactor is to be monitored for high-limit violations. The temperature is measured using a thermocouple that gives a voltage signal in proportion to the temperature. If the temperature exceeds a preset value, an alarm must be turned on and the cooling water supply valve to the jacket must be opened. Both of these are operated using 110 V AC power.

The system can be set up using an interface that provides one digital input and two digital outputs. The schematic of the setup is shown in Figure 4.3. The output from the thermocouple is sent to a comparator that compares it against the preset high-limit voltage. The output of the computer is set to go high (5 V) when the measured temperature exceeds the preset value. This can be sensed through the digital input interface under program control.

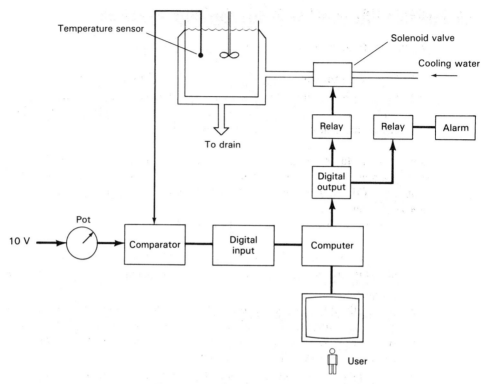

Figure 4.3 Temperature alarm setup

When this input goes high, the two digital outputs can be set high. Two optoisolated relays are necessary since both the alarm and the solenoid valve on the cooling water operate on high-voltage inputs and require significant power.

   The software to drive this system should check if the temperature exceeds the set limit by reading the digital input at a frequency determined by the process requirements. In between the computer can be used for other purposes.

Implementation Using an Apple II Computer

The design of the DAC system for the system just described did not consider any specific hardware or computer. Now consider the situation where we want to accomplish the above using an Apple II. The additional hardware required includes

1. a digital input/output interface card for the Apple II
2. two 110-V relays activated by TTL-level inputs
3. a comparator circuit that will generate a TTL-level signal based on the sensed temperature

The first component cited may be obtained from a number of manufacturers listed at the end of Chapter 5. The last two components are available through electronics suppliers or can be built in-house in an electronics shop.

Let us say we purchased a digital I/O board for the Apple II. These boards will plug into the expansion slots on the motherboard. Each expansion slot has associated with it a set of reserved address locations, as listed here.

Slot no.	Address locations
1	49296–49311
2	49312–49327
3	49328–49343
4	49344–49359
5	49360–49375
6	49376–49391

If the digital I/O card is put in slot 3, we can address it using locations 49318–49335. Thus potentially up to 16 bytes can be transferred through this board.

The number of bits that can be read (output) through the interface board is called the number of input (output) channels. Thus each slot on the Apple has the potential to input (and output) up to $16 \times 8 = 128$ channels. Most commercially available boards allow a small number of channels such as 8 or 16. Note that the input and output are done on separate channels even though they may share the same address location. A byte may be transferred to the output lines using the poke command in BASIC. For example,

$$\text{POKE } 49318, \quad 255$$

will set all output bits on location 49318 to 1 (see Appendix C). Similarly, digital inputs can be read using the PEEK command in BASIC. For example,

$$x = \text{PEEK}(49318)$$

will transfer the 8 bits on the input channels to the location referred to by the variable x. To obtain the status of each line we must decode x further. The decoding can be done using the conversion from decimal to binary. A table of conversions is shown in Appendix C. As an example, a decimal number $x = 128$ can be represented using

Some manufacturers provide subroutine calls to facilitate the reading and outputting of digital I/O channels. For example, commands like

$$\text{I=BIN(slot \#, channel \#)}$$

$$\text{CALL BOUT(value, slot \#, channel \#)}$$

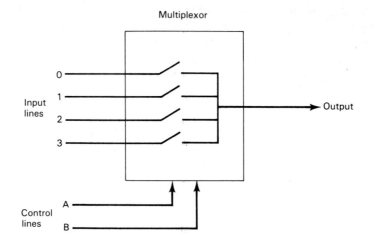

Multiplexor

Input lines
0
1
2
3

Output

Control lines
A
B

Decision Table

A	B	Output connected To input line no.
0	0	Input 0
0	1	Input 1
1	0	Input 2
1	1	Input 3

Figure 4.4   Basic concept of multiplexing

can be constructed to input and output values. Such commands make programming in BASIC easier. Using these commands, a BASIC program to accomplish the objectives of this application will look like the following:

10 I%=BIN(4,1)   :   Read status of digital input on channel 1, slot 4
20 IF (I%=0) GO TO 50
30 CALL BOUT (1,4,1):   Turn on light
40 CALL BOUT (1,4,2):   Turn on alarm
50 GO TO 10   :   Return to read temperature status

This program will endlessly cycle between reading and checking the status. It is possible to set this up as a subroutine that is run every few seconds or so. To do this will require the addition of a real-time clock board to our Apple II computer.

   Another possibility that exists is to set up the program in assembly language and to connect the comparator output to a line called *IRQ* (*interrupt request*) on the CPU bus. The Apple II computer will automatically transfer program control to a certain location in memory whenever this line is activated. This approach is a more efficient way since the computer is then free for other uses and is not constantly tied up reading the digital input channel. However, this requires knowledge of assembly language programming and the way Apple's interrupt line is set up.

Example 2   Multiplexing

Multiplexing is the means by which single output lines can be switched among many possible input lines. Figure 4.4 illustrates the basic concept. There are four input lines and one output line. A specific input line is connected to the output line based on the value of the control lines A and B, as shown in the table associated with the figure.

The concept may be extended to deal with many more inputs. Input lines switched may be analog signals or digital signals. Switching of low-level analog signals is not recommended since the multiplexor will introduce some noise and error to the signal.

Multiplexors are available as semiconductor IC chips. The control lines in this case are TTL compatible. Thus the output of the digital interface may be used to drive the multiplexor.

Multiplexors are used in many applications where an expensive resource must be shared among different input signals.

Figure 4.5 shows one possible application of a multiplexor. Here an expensive amplifier/signal conditioning unit for a resistance thermometer is shared among four temperature sensors. This requires two digital output channels.

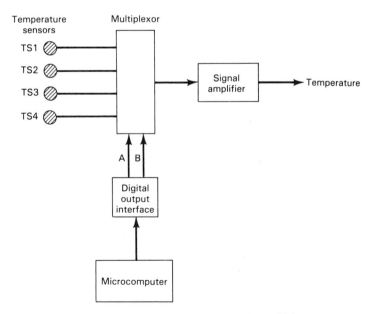

Figure 4.5 Application of digital outputs to switch a multiplexor

Example 3   Digital Power Control

One way to control the power of electric heaters is by controlling the amount of current passing through the heating element. Figure 4.6 shows the voltage across the AC-powered heater wire. The period of the sine wave is 60 cycles/sec. By selecting the number of cycles that are allowed to pass through, the power can be controlled.

Consider the input to such a digital power controller. This controller requires an 8-bit word to determine the power output. If all bits are 0, no power is applied, and full power is applied when all bits are 1.

The control of this device is easily accomplished by directly linking the eight control lines to eight digital output channels. By outputting an 8-bit word to the digital output device, any desired power level can be achieved. For example, to achieve a 50% power level, the following calculation is made:

$$X = \text{INT} (255 \times 0.5)$$
$$= 127$$

Here INT denotes "integer value of." The decimal number 127 can be represented in binary form as 01,111,111. There is no need to do this conversion if it is possible from software to output a decimal integer directly to the digital output interface.

Figure 4.7 shows the schematic of the hardware to drive the power controller. For a detailed description of how such power controllers are constructed and interfaced, the reader is referred to the article by Joseph, Millard, and Elliot listed at the end of this chapter.

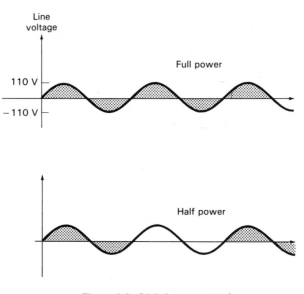

Figure 4.6   Digital power control

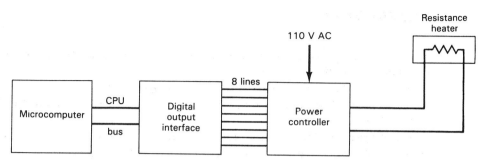

Figure 4.7   Interfacing a digitally controlled resistance heater

SUMMARY

Measurement and control of signals that have only binary states (on/off, up/down, open/closed, high/low, and so on) are classified as digital input/output signals. The interface required consists of two parts: a signal conditioning component that makes the requirements of the process side with the TTL-level signals used in the computer, and a digital interface that enables the device to accept or place data on the CPU bus. The transfer of data is done under software control through user-defined commands. The software may be written in a high-level language such as BASIC or FORTRAN using vendor-supplied subroutines. An alternative is to use a software package that allows the user to operate the input/output device through menu-selected options. The latter is easier to use but not very flexible.

Digital interfaces are comparatively inexpensive and usually come with 8- or 16-channel capability. They can be used in on/off control and to monitor the high/low state of sensor outputs.

REVIEW QUESTIONS

1. What is meant by TTL signals?
2. What type of signal conditioning is required to turn off a 100-W light bulb using a computer?
3. List some of the criteria that you will use in selecting a digital input and digital output interface.
4. What is the meaning of multiplexing? Cite some applications where it can be used.
5. What is the difference between analog multiplexing and digital multiplexing?
6. Design a DAC system for monitoring a house for signs of unauthorized (forced) entry. The system should trigger an alarm and flash some lights in case a forced entry is detected. What kind of interfaces are required?

REFERENCES

The fundamentals of digital signal interfacing along with some do-it-yourself experiments are described in the following two books:

COFFRON, J. W. *The Apple Connection*. Berkeley, CA: Sybex, 1982.

UFFENBECK, J. F. *Hardware Interfacing with the Apple II Plus*. Englewood Cliffs, NJ: Prentice-Hall, 1983.

Aspects of digital interfacing and signal conditioning are discussed in the following excellent books:

HOROWITZ, P., AND W. HILL. *The Art of Electronics*. New York: Cambridge University Press, 1980.

MALMSTADT, H. V., C. G. ENKE, AND S. R. CROUCH. *Electronics and Instrumentation for Scientists*. Menlo Park, CA: Benjamin/Cummings, 1981.

The following article discusses the design and construction of a digital power controller in detail:

JOSEPH, B., D. R. MILLARD, AND D. L. ELLIOT. "Experiments in Temperature Measurement and Control by Microcomputers." *IEEE Control Systems Magazine* 5, no. 3 (August 1985): 26–30.

5

Analog Signal Interfacing

5.1 INTRODUCTION

The majority of signals generated by sensors in the real world fall into the category of analog signals. By analog we mean signals that can take on a continuum of values between upper and lower limits. Figure 5.1 illustrates the difference between analog and digital signals. The accuracy with which the analog signals can be read is limited by the accuracy with which the position of the needle or indicator can be read on the scale. On the other hand, the accuracy of digital display devices is limited by the number of digits used in the display. For example, with a four-digit display on a watch we can only read the hour and minute at any time.

Some measurement devices automatically generate digital signals. Pulse counters, turbine flow meters, scintillation counters, and so on fall into this category. More often than not, however, sensors generate analog signals such as a voltage or a current. If it is desired to measure and sort this sensor output in a computer, then this signal must be converted into digital form first. In digital form, the signal can take on only a finite set of values between its upper and lower limits. This *quantization* of the signal sets an absolute limit on the accuracy (depending on the number of bits used to represent the signal) with which the signal can be measured.

Another aspect of recording analog signals using a computer as opposed to a chart recorder is the finite time sampling dictated by the discrete nature of computer operations. Figure 5.2 illustrates this sampling process. Since the memory of the computer is limited and since the computer operates at finite speed, the signal can be read only at a finite number of points in *time*. This is called the *sampling* process. Sampling necessarily implies some loss of information, since we have no idea what the signal values were in between sampling points. One of our concerns will be how to evaluate and minimize this loss of information.

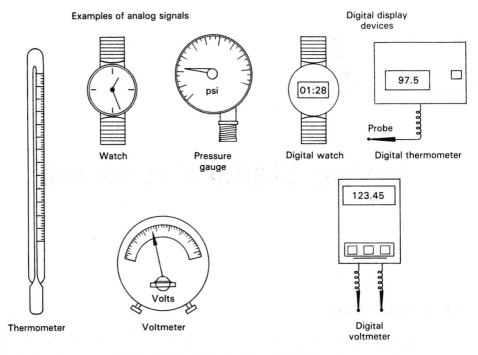

Figure 5.1 Examples of analog and digital signals

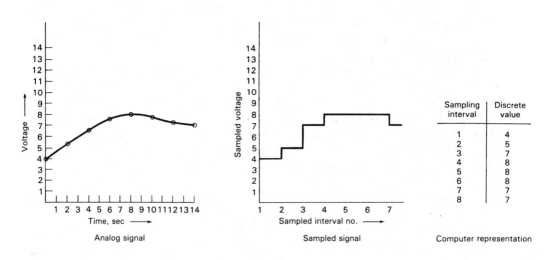

Figure 5.2 Illustrating the sampling and quantization of an analog signal. The sampling interval used is 2 sec.

The majority of measurement sensors generate analog signals. Examples of analog signal generators include

thermocouples

strain gauges

pressure sensors

pH meters

force sensors

level sensors

vortex and differential pressure flow meters

gas chromatographs

spectrophotometers

moisture and humidity sensors

velocity meters

position sensors

The signals generated by the sensors are generally of low voltage and are noisy. Most sensors require some amount of signal amplification, level shift, and noise filtering. These operations, commonly referred to as *signal conditioning,* are the subject of the next chapter. The signal conditioners generate voltage levels in the 0–5 V range. This signal is then converted to digital form using special devices called *analog-to-digital converters (A/D or ADCs).* These devices interface to the bus of the microprocessor. Figure 5.3 illustrates the three steps involved in the analog data acquisition process.

A similar set of steps is involved in the processing of analog output signals. This is also shown in Figure 5.3.

Examples of analog output devices that may be manipulated by the computer include pneumatic control valves and electric power controllers. Such devices require that the computer be able to send a continuous signal to the output device. This is accomplished first by converting the digital output to an analog signal using a *digital-to-analog converter (DAC or D/A)* and then using an appropriate signal conditioning device.

As in the case of digital I/O interfaces, those analog I/O devices operate under

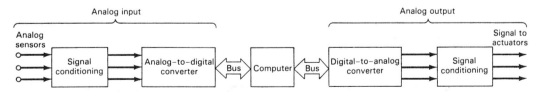

Figure 5.3   Processing of analog input and output signals using a computer

software control. Hence, to read an analog signal, the CPU must be programmed to
execute the following tasks:

1. Send a signal to the A/D converter to sample the current analog input voltage and
   start converting it to digital form.
2. Wait a few microseconds for the conversion to be completed.
3. When the conversion-complete signal is received, read the converted digital value
   that is temporarily stored in the A/D converter.

To output an analog signal, the procedure is reversed. A digital value to be converted is sent to the D/A converter. After the value is converted, the resulting analog voltage
is temporarily stored in a device called a *sample and hold (S/H)*. The output voltage may
then be converted to current or pneumatic signal by the signal conditioner.

These software commands may be generated from machine language code or
through high-level languages such as BASIC or FORTRAN. The manufacturers of analog
interfacing hardware generally provide subroutine libraries (for use with high-level languages) that facilitate the writing of data acquisition software.

This chapter is concerned with the basic principles of sampling and quantizing of
analog signals and the hardware devices used for the purpose. The objective is to provide
you with sufficient background necessary for the selection of appropriate hardware and
software for a given application.

5.2 QUANTIZATION AND SAMPLING

Consider a digital thermometer capable of displaying only two digits. If the thermometer
is set to measure temperatures between 0 and 100°C, the possible readings are

        00
        01
        02
        03
        04
        .
        .
        .
        98
        99

Thus the accuracy is limited to 1°C. A temperature that falls in between will be rounded
off. For example, 91.2 will be displayed as 91, and 91.8 will be displayed as 92 (assum-
ing rounding off to the nearest whole number).

In a computer, analog signals are read and stored as binary integers. First, consider the binary representation of temperatures between 0 and 100°C using a 4-bit binary number. Table 5.1 shows the binary value recorded by the computer and its decimal equivalent for this range of temperatures. As can be seen, only 16 (2^4) different values can be represented using 4-bit binary. This results in an accuracy of $\frac{1}{16} = 6.25\%$ in the measured signal.

TABLE 5.1 QUANTIZATION

Temperature	Binary representation	Decimal equivalent
0–6.24	0000	0
6.25–12.49	0001	1
12.50–18.74	0010	2
18.75–24.99	0011	3
25.00–31.24	0100	4
31.25–37.49	0101	5
37.50–43.74	0110	6
43.75–49.99	0111	7
50.00–56.24	1000	8
56.25–62.49	1001	9
62.50–68.74	1010	10
68.75–74.99	1011	11
75.00–81.24	1100	12
81.25–87.49	1101	13
87.50–93.74	1110	14
93.75–100.00	1111	15

The reconstruction of temperature readings in degrees Celsius from a binary reading is illustrated by the following example. Let

$$A = 1101 \quad \text{(binary)}$$

$$= 13 \quad \text{(decimal)}$$

Then the corresponding temperature is

$$T = \frac{A}{16} \times 100 = \frac{13}{16} \times 100 = 81.25$$

The reconstructed temperature readings will show temperature values that are separated by 6.25°C (0, 6.25, 12.50, 18.75, and so on). No intermediate values will be reported by this device.

Figure 5.4 compares the actual temperature and the temperature obtained after reconstruction from the 4-bit binary representation. Note the staircase nature of the function. Obviously a 4-bit approximation is insufficient for most applications. In practice, 8-, 12-, and 16-bit converters are used. Table 5.2 shows the accuracies obtained with converters using different number of bits. The general rule is that if an n-bit converter is used, then the output will consist of 2^n steps. This will yield an accuracy of $100/2^n\%$. The accuracy is also affected by the output voltage range of the sensor/amplifier combination.

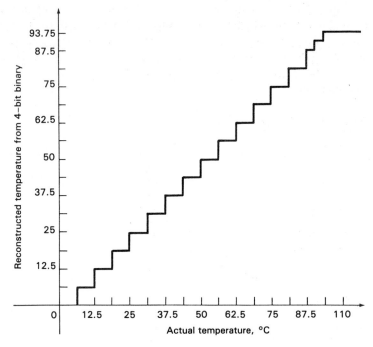

Figure 5.4 Comparison between actual temperature and temperature reconstructed from a 4-bit binary representation

To get maximum accuracy, the output range of the sensor/amplifier should match the input range of the A/D converter.

A/D converters are characterized by the number of bits used in the converted digital representation and the time taken to do the conversion. Generally the cost of an A/D

TABLE 5.2 ACCURACY OF A/D AND D/A CONVERTERS USING DIFFERENT NUMBERS OF BITS

No. of bits	2^n	Percent accuracy
1	2	50
2	4	25
3	8	12.5
4	16	6.25
5	32	3.125
6	64	1.562
7	128	0.781
8	256	0.39
9	512	0.195
10	1024	0.0975
12	4096	0.0244
16	65,536	0.0015

converter increases with the number of bits used and the speed of conversion. In practice a compromise must be achieved between speed, accuracy, and cost.

Commonly used A/D converters provide 12-bit accuracy. This represents an accuracy of 0.024%. The noise components of most signals exceed this percentage. In some special situations, 16-bit converters are used. For analog *outputs,* 8-bit conversion is generally sufficient.

Sampling

Next we turn our attention to another source of error in inputting analog signals into the digital computer. This error, called *sampling error,* arises from discretization of the time variable. Figure 5.5 illustrates the effect of sampling a continuous signal in discrete time. Here we consider a temperature of a tank that is varying with time. On the left is shown an analog record of the temperature variation. On the right are the sampled values of the temperature. Here we have temporarily ignored the discretization error due to quantization of the signal.

If we sample the temperature every 0.5 sec, then a table of temperature values will be generated within the computer. This table is represented as dots in Figure 5.5. In this discrete representation we know nothing about the temperature values at in-between times.

To illustrate this point further and to develop a criterion for selecting the sampling time, consider the sampling of a sinusoidal wave, as illustrated in Figure 5.6. At high sampling frequencies—that is, short sampling times—the original sine wave is almost fully reproduced by the sampled signal as well. As the sampling rate is decreased, the sampled signal begins to look less and less like the original signal. At a sampling

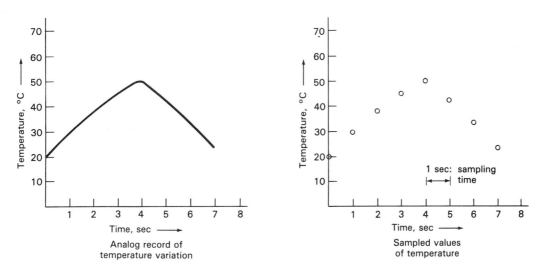

Figure 5.5   Effect of sampling a temperature sensor output

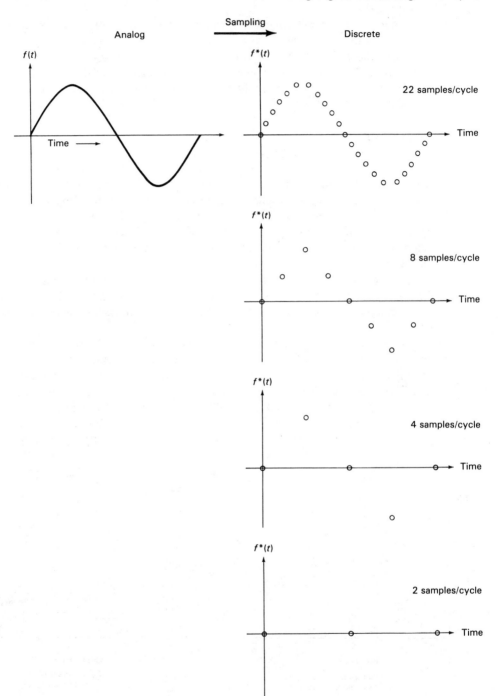

Figure 5.6 Sampling a sine wave at different frequencies

frequency that is four times the frequency of the signal, the sampled signal shows the up-and-down variation. When the sampling frequency is twice the frequency of the sine wave, the signal appears to be constant.

It can be theoretically shown that if the sampling frequency is kept greater than *twice the frequency of the original signal,* then the original signal can be recovered by sampling the signal over a sufficiently long period of time.

Actual signals contain not just one sine wave but a mixture of frequencies. The signal can be thought to be made up of sine waves of different frequencies of varying amplitudes. In such a case the following theorem applies:

Sampling Theorem.   If the highest frequency present in the input signal being sampled is *f,* then in order to be able to reconstruct the signal from the sampled data, it must be sampled at a frequency greater than 2*f.*

Violation of this rule can lead to a phenomenon referred to as *aliasing.* This is illustrated in Figure 5.7. Here a high-frequency signal is sampled at a low frequency. Note that the sampled signal appears to have a frequency of oscillation that is much smaller than the frequency of the original signal being sampled. The frequency of this ''alias'' signal is given by

$$f_{\text{alias}} = f_{\text{actual}} - f_{\text{sample}}$$

Application of the sampling theorem in practice is not easy because it is difficult to determine the frequency content (spectrum) of a signal to be measured. Most often noise levels of frequencies of 50 Hz (cycles/sec) and above are present in the signal. Low-pass filters can be used to remove or reduce the contribution of these high-frequency signal components. The deciding factor is the frequency content of the variable itself, which can be estimated by observing the signal variations in time. A rough rule is to use a sampling frequency at least 10 times the observed frequencies in the signal.

The frequency content of a periodic signal can be analyzed using special instru-

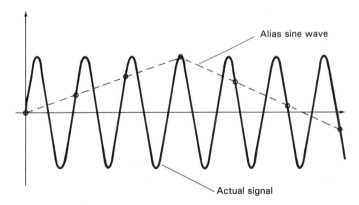

Figure 5.7   Illustrating the concept of aliasing

ments called *spectral analyzers*. Another approach is to sample the signal at a very high rate (as high as possible) and then use one of the standard software packages for fast Fourier transform (FFT). This will yield the amplitude of high-frequency components present in the signal. At some frequency these amplitudes will begin to tail off. The low-amplitude sine wave components will not have much effect on the sampling process. The sampling frequency should be such that the amplitudes of the sinusoids present at half the sampling frequency are small enough to be ignored. If high-frequency noise components are present in the signal, then these noise components should be filtered out before sampling to prevent aliasing errors. Filtering techniques are discussed in Chapter 6.

5.3 HARDWARE FOR A/D AND D/A CONVERSION

The hardware necessary for A/D and D/A conversion generally comes in the form of boards that interface with the expansion slots on the motherboard of the microcomputer. The hardware manufacturers also provide the software drivers necessary to input or output data through these boards. In this section, we will discuss some of the technology used and the specifications used and options available with A/D and D/A boards.

Technology of A/D and D/A Conversion

D/A converters are simpler to construct and hence we will discuss these first. The basic function of the D/A converter is to take a binary number and produce a voltage in proportion to this number. The number of bits used in the converter is called the *resolution* of the converter. D/A conversion is accomplished using a ladder network of precision resistors. The current flowing through the resistors is adjusted by opening and closing switches based on the input binary number. Thus the circuit generates a voltage proportional to the input binary number.

In contrast with the D/A conversion technology, there are a number of different technologies for doing the reverse operation: A/D conversion. The three basic types of A/D converters are

1. integrating
2. feedback
3. parallel or flash

Integrating-type converters are based on charging up a capacitor with a series of pulses of known charge until the capacitor is charged up to the unknown input voltage that is to be converted into a binary number. The number of pulses required are counted and this count then forms the binary representation of the unknown input voltage. *Dual-slope integrating converters* first charge the capacitor to the unknown input voltage and then measure the time taken to discharge the capacitor at a set rate. This approach results in better accuracy.

Feedback- or servo-type converters are based on guessing a binary number, converting this to a voltage using a D/A converter, and then comparing the voltages to the unknown input voltage. The process is repeated until the output of the D/A converter equals the unknown input voltage, at which point we have correctly guessed the equivalent binary representation. Various types of search strategies are used in the feedback-type converters, the most common being the successive approximation approach. The advantage of the feedback-type converters is their speed. But they are not as accurate as the integrating-type converters.

The fastest type of A/D converters are the parallel or flash converters. These employ multiple sets of comparator circuits to determine each bit of the binary representation separately. These are not commonly used because of their high cost.

Conversion times of A/D converters range from a few nanoseconds for the flash-type converters to a few milliseconds for the integrating-type converters. Conversion times of a few microseconds are common for the feedback-type converters.

Choices Available

The choices available with the A/D and D/A boards are many. We will discuss a few of the important ones.

1. Resolution.   This is the number of bits used to represent the binary equivalent of the input or output voltage. Common choices here are 8-, 12-, or 16-bit. Most applications require at least 12-bit accuracy on the input side and 8-bit accuracy for the outputs.

2. Number of channels.   The number of input channels represents the number of different input signal sources that may be tied to that A/D board. Most board manufacturers provide for 8 or 16 input channels and 2 to 4 output channels. Presumably there is more demand for input channels than output channels. Each channel may have its own D/A converter, or all channels may share a common A/D converter (this being an expensive component). In the latter case, the channels are multiplexed internally on the board. This means that only one channel may be read at any one time, and that scanning all channels will take much longer than taking data from a single channel.

3. Signal conditioning.   Some A/D boards are set up to accept signals directly from sensors such as thermocouples, RTD devices, and strain gauges. These boards contain the necessary amplification, filtering, and level shifting needed before the conversion of the signal to digital form.

4. Input and output voltage levels.   The acceptable input voltage levels for the signal lines connected to the A/D channels is specified as a range. Typical ranges are 0 to 10 V, -10 to 10 V, -5 to 5 V, 0 to 5 V, 0 to 100 mV, and 0 to 10 mV. Some boards allow the range to be switch selectable. The accuracy of the voltage reading will depend on the input range. As an example, an 8-bit converter with an input range of 0 to 5 V implies that the digital data read will go from 0 to 255 as the voltage goes from 0 to 5 V. Thus the resolution is 5/255 V.

Another input/output option is the industry standard 4–20 mA current.

5. Programmable gain.   Programmable gain implies that the input voltage range may be selected by the software. This allows a programmer to read low-level voltages with greater accuracy. The programmer must first send a message to the A/D board to set the gain and then ask for the conversion to start.

6. Single-ended versus differential input channels.   Single-ended channels use a single wire to carry the signal. The voltage level is measured with respect to the ground of the computer. This makes the signal susceptible to common mode noise (see Chapter 6). Greater noise immunity is obtained by using differential input channels, which take the voltage difference between two lines and then convert this to digital value.

7. Direct memory access (DMA).   High-speed data acquisition can be accomplished using this feature. DMA is used to refer to the ability of the board to send data directly to memory without going through the CPU. Once initiated, data transfer takes place automatically. Sampling rates of 50,000 samples/sec and higher can be achieved through this method. The DMA controller utilizes idle periods between program instructions to get control of the bus and transfer data to memory. Tape drives and disk drives often use this technique to achieve high data transfer rates.

8. Plug-in boards versus external boxes.   Plug-in boards go directly into the expansion slots of the computer and cost less. External boxes are connected to the computer's bus through a card in the expansion slot and allow the user to purchase and install many different types of I/O boards. The latter would be useful if the number of input and output signals is large (most have a maximum of 16 input channels).

9. Scanning.   This refers to the ability to automatically scan and read inputs from all channels.

A/D Specifications

The important variables used to specify the operating capabilities of an A/D converter are described next.

1. Power consumption.   This is the power required to operate the board. Plug-in boards draw their power from the power supply of the computer itself. External boxes often have their own separate power supply.

2. Resolution.   Resolution refers to the number of bits used in the conversion. For bipolar inputs a sign bit may be additionally specified.

3. Accuracy.   Accuracy is a measure of the error in representing the voltage as a number. Typical specification is 0.01% of full-scale reading.

4. Full scale.   This refers to the maximum and minimum input voltage.

5. Common mode rejection.   Expressed as decibels. This refers to the ratio by which common mode voltage is reduced from input to output. A ratio of 60 db means a reduction by a factor of 10^{-3}.

6. Linearity.   This indicates the extent to which there is a linear relationship between input voltage and the converted digital output, usually ± 1 bit.

7. Monotonicity.   For a continuously increasing input voltage, the digital output should also increase continuously. Any deviation from this is expressed as the error in monotonicity.

8. Zero and gain drift.   Changes in output for zero input, with temperature. Typically 1 $\mu V/°C$.

9. Conversion time.   This is the time required to complete an A/D conversion. It usually refers to the time required by the A/D converter chip. In practice, the time also depends on the software used. Highest rates are achievable in assembly language coding. Typical rates achievable from BASIC on an IBM PC are 30 samples/sec for low-speed boards to 4000 samples/sec for high-speed boards. Speeds up to 50,000 samples/sec are achievable with boards having DMA capability.

5.4 APPLICATIONS

Temperature Logging of a Distillation Unit

A distillation column in a pilot plant setup is instrumented with 24 thermocouples. Currently a few selected thermocouples are connected to a temperature logging instrument, which records the temperatures on a strip chart recorder. It is desired to automate the data collection process using a microcomputer.

The temperatures range from 50 to 200°C and should be recorded with ± 1°C accuracy. An analysis of the previous temperature records indicates that the temperatures may show oscillations with frequencies as low as 1 cycle/min.

Problem analysis.   The percent accuracy requirement is calculated first:

$$\text{Percent accuracy} = \frac{1}{200 - 50} \times 100 = 0.66$$

Comparing this to Table 5.2, we conclude that an 8-bit converter would be barely adequate.

The lowest frequency of the sampled signal suggests that a sampling frequency of 10/min be used. This is fairly slow and can be achieved by using programs written in high-level languages.

The number of points (24) to be sampled is very large. Most commercial analog input hardware does not accept this many channels. Also, since the thermocouples produce only low-level signals in the millivolt range, signal conditioning is required.

One possible solution to this problem is to use a multiplexor to switch between the channels that share a common signal conditioning unit. This calls for digital outputs from the computer to switch the channels (see Example 2 in Section 4.4).

DAC system.   Figure 5.8 shows the DAC system design. A common signal conditioning unit and analog input channel is used to read all 24 thermocouples. To switch among the 24 thermocouples, 5 digital outputs are used. Sampling is done in sequence. This will result in a small time difference in the times at which the thermocouples are sampled.

The software requirements for the DAC system are as follows. Every 6 sec the temperatures should be read. To sample each channel, the appropriate digital number should be sent to the multiplexor through the digital output device and the A/D converter requested to start the conversion process. After the conversion is complete, the value is read and temporarily stored in memory. After all the values are read, further processing such as data conversion, printing, display, and disk storage may be done. The entire operation is repeated every 6 sec.

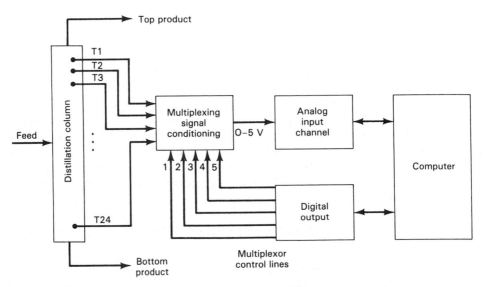

Figure 5.8 DAC system for temperature logging

Temperature Control of a Heated Bar

A metal bar is heated at one end using a resistance heating element. It is desired to monitor the temperature profile in the bar and to control the temperature at one end by manipulating the power input into the heating element.

The temperature profile is monitored by means of five thermistor heads embedded in the metal rod. The resistance of these thermistor heads changes with temperature according to a resistance-versus-temperature chart provided by the thermistor manufacturer. The resistance is measured by passing a known current and observing the voltage drop across the thermistor. A voltage drop in the range of 0.1 to 0.2 V is obtained over the temperatures of interest (0–100°C).

Since the voltages to be measured are small, an analog input board that can accept voltages in this range is desirable. If we use an A/D converter that can read 0–0.2 V input with a 12-bit converter, the accuracy obtained will be

$$\frac{0.2 \text{ V}}{4096 \text{ bits}}$$

A 100°C change causes a change of 0.1 V. Hence

$$\text{Accuracy} = \frac{0.2 \text{ V}}{4096 \text{ bits}} \times \frac{100°C}{0.1 \text{ V}} = 0.05°C/\text{bit}$$

Power input to the resistance heater may be controlled by a power controller that will accept 0–5 V input and produce a proportional power. Because of high voltages in the power circuit, a galvanic isolation of the unit is desirable. Power can be controlled using an analog output channel. If, for example, an analog output channel with 0–10 V output capability and a 12-bit converter is used, the accuracy attainable in power control is estimated as follows:

$$\text{Accuracy of power control} = \frac{10 \text{ V}}{4096 \text{ bits}} \times \frac{100\% \text{ power}}{5 \text{ V}}$$

Thus power may be controlled to within 0.05%.

This assumes that the power control device is linear. Nonlinearities in the power controller can reduce this accuracy. For nonlinear devices the calculation should be done using the maximum slope of the power-versus-input voltage curve of the power controller.

The required sampling rate can be estimated by first determining the response time of the rod to temperature changes in input power. Make a step increase in the power input and observe how fast the temperature rises. The time required to attain 63% of the final temperature is the time constant of the system. The sampling time should be kept smaller than $\frac{1}{10}$ of this time constant.

DAC system.   Figure 5.9 shows the resulting DAC system. Since the number of temperatures to be measured is small, it is possible to use an 8-channel analog input card.

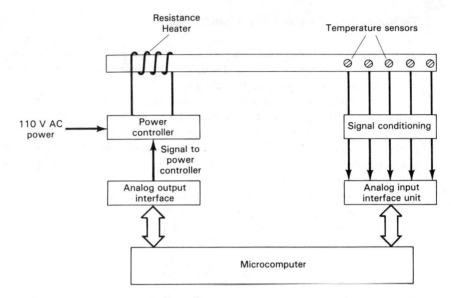

Figure 5.9   Temperature control of a metal rod

One analog output channel is also required. Some signal conditioning is necessary to generate the current for the thermistors and measure the voltage drop across it.

Software should convert the value read by the analog input channel into a temperature. A table of values read by the channel versus temperature may be created and stored on a disk a priori to aid this conversion.

The control algorithms needed to control the temperatures by manipulating the power input to the resistance heater must also be incorporated in the software. Control algorithms are discussed in more detail in Chapter 8.

SUMMARY

In this chapter we looked at the difference between analog and digital representation and the hardware used to convert from one to the other. The digitization of a signal automatically introduces errors due to quantization and sampling. The sampling theorem puts a lower limit on the sampling rate of a given signal. Quantization error is dependent on the number of bits used to represent the analog signal.

The choices available with A/D and D/A systems were discussed. Popular microcomputers have a wider range of hardware interfaces available in the market. Improvements in hardware technology have led to a marked decrease in the cost of such interface boards. Some manufacturers of interface boards are listed at the end of this chapter.

REVIEW QUESTIONS

1. Give several examples of analog signals and digital signals.

2. How does one quantify the error due to quantization? How many bits are required to represent a temperature in the range 0–10°C?

3. What is the recommended sampling rate for a signal having frequency components as high as 10 Hz?

4. How does one deal with the high-frequency noise components present in a signal?

5. What is the meaning of number of channels in a D/A converter? What is a differential input channel?

6. Contact a few manufacturers listed at the end of this chapter and obtain specifications for A/D and D/A boards available for your choice of a microcomputer. Compare the specifications.

7. What is the meaning of conversion time for a D/A converter?

8. List three types of A/D converters on the market today. Which is the fastest? Most accurate?

9. What is DMA? Where is it useful?

10. What is a programmable gain A/D converter? Where is it useful?

REFERENCES

VanDoren, A. *Data Acquisition Systems*. Reston, VA: Reston, 1982.
  This is an excellent book that explains the technology of A/D and D/A conversion. It includes a clear description of all the sources of error in data acquisition using a computer. It also explains in detail the terminology used in specifying A/D and D/A conversion systems.

Mellichamp, D. A., ed. *Real-Time Computing with Applications to Data Acquisition and Control*. New York: Van Nostrand Reinhold, 1983.
  This book contains a chapter on analog and digital interfacing.

Stone, H. S. *Microcomputer Interfacing*. Reading, MA: Addison-Wesley, 1982.
  The above book has sections on DMA explaining what it is and how it is done.

Uffenbeck, J. E. *Hardware Interfacing Using the IBM-PC*. Englewood Cliffs, NJ: Prentice-Hall, 1983.
  This book is good for people interested in learning to build interface boards. It takes you step by step through various projects. Uffenbeck has written books like this for other computers as well. Another similar book is the following:

Coffron, J. W. *The Apple Connection*, Berkeley, CA: Sybex, 1982.

LIST OF MANUFACTURERS

The following is a partial listing of manufacturers that market hardware and software for analog and digital signal interfacing. Complete addresses are given in Appendix B.

Acrosystems Corp.

Action Instruments

Analog Devices

Burr-Brown Corp.

Cyber Research, Inc.

Cyborg Corp.

Data Acquisition Systems

Data Translation

Digital Equipment Corp.

Elexor

GW Instruments

Hamilton

Hewlett-Packard

Interactive Microwave, Inc.

Interactive Structures, Inc.

Keithly Data Acquisition and Control, Inc.

Metrabyte Corp.

Motorola Semiconductor Products, Inc.

Mountain Computer, Inc.

National Instruments

Omega Engineering, Inc.

Qua Tech, Inc.

Scientific Solutions, Inc.

Starbuck Data Co.

Strawberry Tree Computers

Taurus Computer Products, Inc.

6

Sensors and Signal Conditioning

6.1 INTRODUCTION

A great deal of preliminary processing goes on before a measurement gets to the computer interface. Figure 6.1 shows the possible processing steps. The first component is the *sensor* itself. The sensor is a device capable of responding in a predetermined way to the actual physical variable being measured. The signal generated by the sensor may be either electrical or mechanical. This signal must be converted to a form suitable for transmission over to the computer, which may be located nearby or far away. At the other end, the transmitted signal must be received and converted to a form acceptable to the analog-to-digital converter. The types of signal transformation required include

Amplification: raising the strength of the signal

Filtering: removing an undesirable portion of the signal

Level shifting: adding a bias voltage to the signal

Linearization: linearizing a signal that changes in a nonlinear fashion

Signal conversion: changing from voltage to current, current to voltage, pressure to current, and so on

From the point of view of designing a DAC system, it is desirable to sense the variable as accurately as possible within the cost bounds set for the system. The accuracy achievable is strongly dependent on the system configuration and the choice of various signal conditioning elements. The purpose of this chapter is to provide a bird's-eye view of this vast field of signal conditioning with specific emphasis on how to eliminate or minimize the sources of error in the measurement of the variable.

Some manufacturers of computer interfaces provide signal conditioning circuitry for

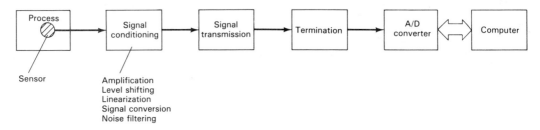

Figure 6.1   Signal processing steps

commonly used sensors. However, the majority of interfaces expect some signal conditioning to have taken place before the signal arrives at the computer interface. In any case, an awareness of the signal transformation that goes on in these signal conditioning units can help you make more judicious selection among the various possibilities.

6.2 SENSORS

Sensors (or transducers, as they are sometimes called) come in two types. *Passive* sensors use energy from the measured variable to generate an output signal. Generally, the signal thus generated is very weak. Examples of sensors in this category include thermocouples, photoelectric devices, and electrodes. *Active* sensors, on the other hand, use an excitation current to enhance the sensitivity of the device. This allows an extra degree of freedom in the design of the sensor signal conditioning device. Examples of active sensors include RTDs (resistance temperature devices) and strain gauges.

Characteristics to look for in a sensor include the useful range of operation and the sensitivity of the device to the variable being measured. Linearity is a useful characteristic but is not always achievable. For a linear sensor the sensor output is linearly related to the sensor input. Nonlinearity leads to changing sensitivity; that is, the device will be more accurate in one region than another. If a nonlinear sensor is used, then this nonlinear

TABLE 6.1   SOME SENSORS AND THEIR CHARACTERISTICS

Sensor	Measured variable	Characteristics
Thermocouple	Temperature	Uses voltage generated by the junction of two metals at different temperatures. This is a passive device. Output is a nonlinear function.
Thermistor and RTDs	Temperature	Uses the changes in resistance with temperature. Active device. Resistance is measured using a Wheatstone bridge. RTDs have good linearity over wide ranges.
Strain gauge	Pressure, liquid level, weight	Uses the change in resistance due to changes in the applied pressure.
Semiconductor	Temperature	Based on changes in the characteristics of a semiconductor device with temperature. Requires excitation voltage or current. Limited operating range.

relationship between the sensor output and the measured variable must be known a priori (it should be provided by the manufacturer).

Table 6.1 lists some commonly used sensors, the property they measure, and their characteristics.

The common problem with all sensors is how to separate the signal from any extraneous noise. This is particularly true of low-energy-level signals. At signal levels of a few millivolts, noise induced by radio frequency interference, by temperature variations, and so on can be significant. The section on noise filtering deals with this aspect in more detail.

The key features to look for in selecting a sensor are the span (the maximum and minimum values of the variable over which the sensor is guaranteed to work) and the accuracy. Accuracy can be expressed in many ways. The following are typical.

1. accuracy expressed in terms of the measured variable, for example, $\pm$ 1°F, $\pm$ 0.5 psi
2. accuracy expressed as a percent of span, for example, $\pm$ 1% of span
3. accuracy expressed as a percentage of actual output reading, for example, $\pm$ 1 mV

6.3 SIGNAL CONDITIONING

Signal Amplification

The low-level signals generated by the sensors must be amplified before transmission to the computer. Amplifier circuits are built up using integrated chips known as *operational amplifiers* (*opamps*).

Amplifiers are characterized by the following quantities (among others):

Gain: This is defined as the change in output for a unit change in input. Amplifier gains can be as high as 1000 using a single stage. Gain is adjustable by changing a resistance.

Bias: This is defined as the output voltage when the input is zero. This represents a shift in the variable. The bias is also an adjustable quantity.

Amplifiers are active devices and require a power source to operate. Although amplifiers behave linearly over most of the input range, all amplifiers exhibit some nonlinearity.

Differential amplifiers take the voltage difference between two input lines and amplify this difference. This is useful when the grounds with respect to which the voltage is measured in the sensor circuitry are different from the ground in the amplifier. The use of a differential amplifier is illustrated in Figure 6.2. Note that in the case of the single-input amplifier, the difference in voltage between the two grounds will lead to a current loop. This loop will cause errors in the amplifier output. For this reason it is preferable to use differential amplifiers when measuring low-level input signals.

Amplifiers are also characterized by their response times. As with any real device, it takes a finite time to respond fully to changes in inputs. Typically this time is measured in

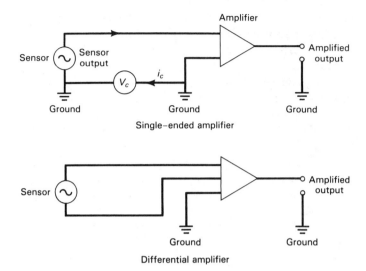

Figure 6.2 Single-ended versus differential amplifier

nanoseconds. For variables that change at much slower rates, this creates no problem. Only when measuring fast-changing variables should this be a major consideration in amplifier selection.

Instrumentation amplifiers are high-accuracy devices built specially for processing sensor output signals. While these are expensive, they offer good noise rejection and linearity characteristics.

For commonly used sensors, many instrument manufacturers offer packaged signal conditioning units. These can be purchased with gain and bias adjustments and a built-in filter to remove noise in the measurement.

Isolation

Another feature that is available with some amplifiers is input isolation. This refers to the elimination of direct metallic contact between the circuitry of the input and the output. This is generally accomplished by providing an optical link between the input and output or by using transformers. The idea is to prevent high voltages from one side passing on to the other and causing damage. Isolation up to several thousand volts can be provided. Such isolation might be required in situations where the presence of high voltages can be harmful (for example, if the output from the amplifier is sent to a computer).

Multiplexing

Because of the high cost associated with signal conditioning units, it is sometimes preferable to share such devices among many sensors. This is accomplished using *multiplexors*, as illustrated in Figure 6.3. The multiplexor will require control input lines to select the

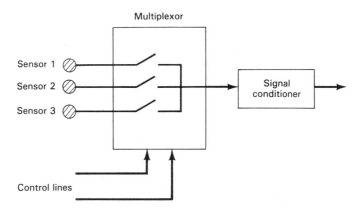

Figure 6.3   Sharing of signal conditioner among sensors

desired sensor. There are also multiplexors that operate sequentially, selecting each sensor in order. The price paid for this is the increased time required to sample all sensors.

Programmable Gain Amplifiers

Programmable gain amplifiers are sometimes provided with analog-to-digital interface devices. As the name implies, the gain of the amplifier may be selected by the user by means of software commands. There is a choice of three or four gains (1, 10, 100, and so on) that the user sets before sampling a signal.

Programmable gain amplifiers offer versatility by being able to adapt to varying signal processing applications.

6.4 NOISE SOURCES AND PREVENTION

All measurements are corrupted by noise from various sources. Thus

$$\text{Measured variable} = \text{signal} + \text{noise}$$

In this section we consider various sources of noise in the measurement, how to reduce or eliminate these noise sources, and finally how to filter out the noise from the measurement.

Noise levels are characterized by the *signal-to-noise ratio (S/N ratio)*, defined as

$$\text{SNR} = \text{S/N} = \frac{\text{average signal level}}{\text{root mean square (rms) noise}} = \frac{V_s}{V_n}$$

Sometimes this is expressed in decibels (db):

$$\text{SNR (db)} = 10 \log_{10} (V_s^2 / V_n^2)$$

Noise can be induced by the sensing instrument or by electromagnetic interference during transmission. Instrument-related noise arises from temperature variations, improper grounding, and from noisy power supply lines. The quality of integrated circuit chips used plays a significant role in determining the extent of instrument-induced noise. Commonly used amplifiers induce noise levels of 50–100 db.

Thermally induced noise is caused by *emf* (*electromotive force*) generated from metal junctions at different temperatures. This can be reduced by minimizing temperature variations within the instrument.

Improper grounding can lead to ground loops of the type shown earlier in Figure 6.2. The difference in voltage between the two grounds is called the *common mode voltage* and the noise induced by this is called the *common mode error*. Voltages should not be measured with respect to ground unless all the grounds used in the instrument are maintained at the same level.

Electromagnetic interference can be reduced by proper shielding of cables and instruments. There are several types of shielded cables available. Coaxial cables consist of a single conducting wire and shield. The outer shield is used as a signal ground. Sometimes this can lead to common mode noise arising from fluctuations in the ground voltage levels between the transmission point and the receiving end. It may be preferable to use a shielded twisted-pair cable that has two conductors twisted around each other. The twisting reduces the amount of electromagnetically induced noise. Signals up to 1 MHz frequency can be transmitted using this type of cable. The shield should be grounded only at one end, to prevent a current from flowing through the shield.

Cables carrying low-level signals should be separated from power lines to the extent possible. The 60 Hz noise from AC power lines and 120 Hz noise from fluorescent lamps are major sources of noise.

The high-speed switching of signals that takes place in digital communication lines is another source of electromagnetic interference. For this reason any low-level lines carried inside the computer should be provided with sufficient protection (shielding). The circuitry used for amplifying these low-level signals should also be shielded.

Sources of high-frequency electromagnetic noise, such as the digital lines carrying signals from the computer to the video display, should also have sufficient shielding to prevent noise interference in low-level lines.

Signal Transmission

Signal quality deteriorates with transmission distance. For this reason it is preferable to locate the signal conditioning circuitry at the signal source itself and then transmit high-level signals.

Since voltage levels tend to drop with distance, current loops are preferred when transmitting signals over distances of more than a few feet. Here a voltage-to-current converter is used to generate a current typically in the range 4–20 mA. Signals may be transmitted over several hundred feet in this manner.

Another possibility is to convert the signal to digital form before transmission. An A/D converter is used to generate the digital signal. Digital signals are not subject to noise interference problems like analog signals because of the high tolerances allowed in the signal level. Some manufacturers offer the circuitry necessary for this conversion. The transmission of digital signals is discussed in Chapter 10.

A choice of two-wire and four-wire transmitters is available. Two-wire transmitters use the current loop also as a source of power for the active devices in the transmitter. Some accuracy is lost this way. Four-wire transmitters have separate lines for carrying power to the transmitter and for carrying the signal.

6.5 NOISE FILTERING

Now we consider the possible ways of recovering the original signal from a measurement corrupted by noise. This is known as *noise filtering*. Noise filtering may be done with the analog signal itself or after the signal has been converted to digital form.

Filtering is accomplished by removing certain frequency components of the measurement. Analog filters are typically made of capacitors and resistances. *Passive* filters operate using the power contained in the signal itself. *Active* filters are more expensive and require an external power supply to operate.

Filters are characterized by the frequency ranges removed by the filtering operation. Figure 6.4 shows a simple RC filter and its frequency response. The frequency response is

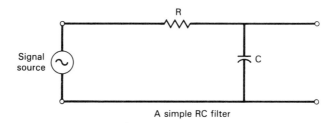

A simple RC filter

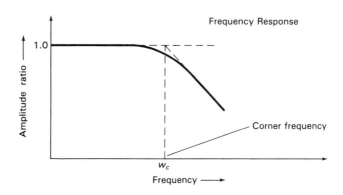

Figure 6.4   A simple RC filter and its frequency response

obtained as follows. A pure sinusoidal wave is input to the filter and the amplitude of the output sine wave is noted. From this, an *amplitude ratio* (*AR*) is computed as follows:

$$AR = \frac{\text{amplitude of output sine wave}}{\text{amplitude of input sine wave}}$$

For the filter shown, the AR = 1 for low frequencies, which means that such signals pass through the filter without any effect. At high frequencies, the AR drops off sharply, and so high-frequency components do not pass through this filter. Such a filter is called a *low-pass* filter and is characterized by the corner frequency (cutoff frequency).

Most electromagnetically induced noise tends to be in higher frequencies and as a result, this type of filter is useful in removing such noise. Recall that high-frequency components can lead to aliasing when sampled at low frequencies. Thus it is advisable to have high-frequency noise removed prior to sampling.

Figure 6.5 shows three ideal filters. At the top the ideal *low-pass* filter is shown. In

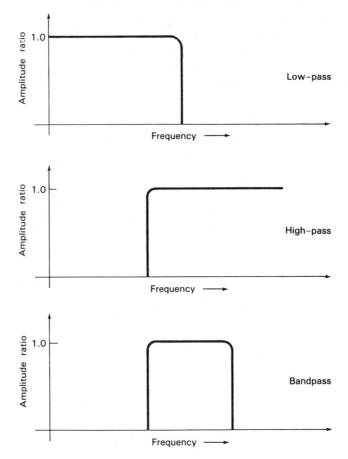

Figure 6.5   Three types of ideal filters

practice, this sharp cutoff is not achievable. If only the high-frequency portion of the signal is of interest, a *high-pass* filter might be used. This is shown in the middle on Figure 6.5. At the bottom a *bandpass* filter (which passes only a fixed band of frequencies) is shown. The low-pass filter is the most commonly used variety.

All filters introduce a certain lag in the signal. This means that the output will be slightly delayed with respect to the input. This time lag becomes larger at high frequencies. Filters using inductance-capacitance (LC) circuits introduce smaller lags but cost more.

Digital Filtering

It is also possible to reduce the noise in a signal by filtering after the signal has been sampled and digitized. This is known as *digital filtering*.

The simplest form of digital filtering is *signal averaging*. Hence, multiple readings of a signal are taken over closely spaced time intervals during which the signal is not expected to vary much. The average of these values then provides a filtered value of the signal. Since most naturally induced noise is random in nature, the averaging will reduce the contribution of this random noise component. It does not remove any steady noise component (noise that is constant over the sampling period).

Digital filters that behave like low-pass analog filters can be designed in this way. Let $X_1, X_2, X_3, \ldots, X_n$ be the noisy data sequence. Then a filtered sequence of signals can be generated as follows:

$$Y_i = aY_{i-1} + (1-a)X_i$$

$$\text{with } Y_0 = X_0$$

With $a = 0$, no filtering takes place. With $a = 1$, all input data is filtered out. When a is between 0 and 1, filtering action with various cutoff frequencies occurs. As in the analog filter, this low-pass filter will introduce a lag in the signal being sampled.

The above filter is called a *first-order filter* since only one previous value of Y is used. A *second-order filter* may be obtained by combining two first-order filters in sequence one after the other, perhaps with differing filter constants. A second-order filter will exhibit a sharper dropoff curve in the frequency response. It is possible to construct even higher-order filters. The use of a first-order filter is illustrated using a sine wave signal in Figure 6.6. Shown in the figure are the original sine wave signal, the signal after a 15% random noise has been added to it, and the result of applying a first-order filter with $a = 0.5$. As can be seen, the filter smooths out the variations but introduces a lag in the signal. In this case the noise was present in frequencies close to the actual frequency of the signal, and a first-order noise filter alone is not able to remove the noise without a high value for a. The first-order filter works best in removing high-frequency components of the noise signal.

Another form of filter is the *moving average filter*, which removes noise by taking the average of the last few samples taken. That is,

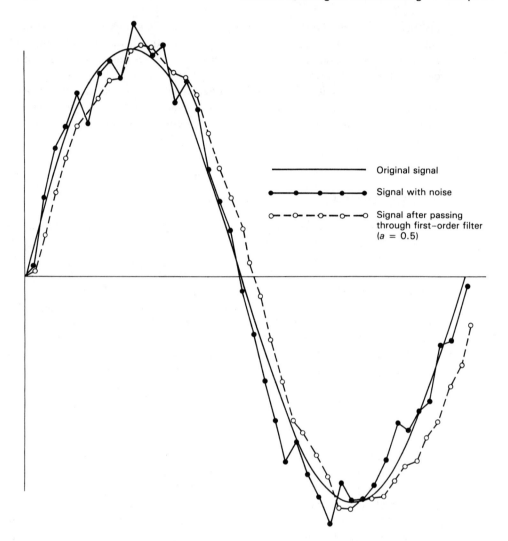

Figure 6.6 Graph showing the effect of digital filtering on a noisy sine wave

$$Y_i = X_i + X_{i-1} + X_{i-2} + \ldots + X_{i-k}/(k + 1)$$

where X_i is the new data and Y_i is the filtered data. As k gets large the output will filter out a greater fraction of the input.

A different approach to filtering is based on *frequency spectrum analysis*. The frequency spectrum of a signal can be obtained by using electronic hardware called frequency spectrum analyzers or by employing software (after the signal has been sampled) using packages for fast Fourier transform (FFT). The Fourier spectrum will provide the amplitude of each frequency present in the signal. A portion of the frequency attributable to the noise can be removed and the remainder converted back into the time domain to obtain a signal without noise. Care should be taken to sample the signal at a fast enough rate to include all frequencies present (see the sampling theorem stated in the previous chapter).

As mentioned earlier, most signal transmitters incorporate some form of analog filtering on the signal. This may be followed by additional digital filtering after the data has been sampled. Some trial and error may be required to determine the best values for the filter constants.

SUMMARY

In this chapter we covered some basic ground related to measuring a variable and transmitting it to the computer. Most sensors generate very low-energy outputs, which must be amplified prior to digitizing. Signal conditioning may also involve linearization, analog filtering, and voltage-current conversion. One important element here is the externally induced noise that can corrupt the signal being measured. Good grounding and shielding can minimize the noise in the signal. Noise can be removed by analog and/or digital filtering. But filtering can introduce a lag in the signal and can also remove a portion of the signal itself.

REVIEW QUESTIONS

1. What is the difference between active and passive sensors?
2. What is common mode voltage? What is its significance in the measurement of a signal?
3. Explain the following terms:
   (a) optical isolation
   (b) differential amplifier
   (c) gain
   (d) bias
4. How does one implement a low-pass filter in software?
5. Explain the difference between analog filtering and digital filtering.
6. What is a Fourier transform? Show how it can be used to remove noise from a signal.
7. When does one use a multiplexor?
8. What are the advantages of using current to transmit a signal as opposed to a voltage?
9. What is electromagnetic interference? How can it be minimized?

REFERENCES

The following is a valuable reference for selecting sensors and instrumentation:

LIPTAK, B. G., ED. *Instrument Engineers Handbook, Process Measurements.* rev. ed. Radnor, PA: Chilton, 1982.

The book by Horowitz and Hill is a good starting point for those interested in how the signal conditioning circuits are built. It also contains a good discussion on grounding and shielding practices.

HOROWITZ, P., AND W. HILL *The Art of Electronics.* New York: Cambridge University Press, 1980.

MALMSTADT, H. V., C. G. ENKE, AND S. R. CROUCH. *Electronics and Instrumentation for Scientists.* Menlo Park, CA: Benjamin/Cummings, 1981.

The following work discusses many practical tips for transducer interfacing:

SHEINGOLD, D. M. *Transducer Interfacing Handbook.* Norwood, MA: Analog Devices, 1981.

The Instrument Society of America puts out a directory every year listing products, manufacturers, trade names, and addresses:

ISA. *Directory of Instrumentation.* Research Triangle Park, NC: Instrument Society of America (published yearly).

7

Real-Time Programming

7.1 INTRODUCTION

In Chapter 3, we discussed the characteristics of general-purpose software that came with microcomputer systems. The specific requirements of DAC systems are a subset of the field of computing known as real-time computing. Here we are concerned with performing calculations according to external events. The program sequence that needs to be executed is tied to the information the computer receives from the sensors and switches interfaced to the computer.

The way this is accomplished is by dividing the program into independently executable modules called *tasks*. A task is similar to a subroutine except that a task does not call another task, although a task might request that another task be activated. This leads to a concept called *multitasking*, which is a primary distinguishing feature of *real-time operating systems* (*RTOS*).

Multitasking should be distinguished from multiprogramming, which refers to the ability of the computer to run more than one program simultaneously (as it appears to the user). In reality even in a multiprogramming environment only one program has control of the CPU at any one time. But a program may be stopped before completion and yield control of the CPU to another program upon the user's demand. The stopped program may then be resumed whenever the user wishes to do so.

By providing a layered view of the screen (one layer for each program being run), it is possible to view the current status of each program being run. This is called *windowing*.

The difference between multitasking and multiprogramming is that in multiprogramming the programs are not related to each other and can run to completion on their own. In a multitasking environment, the multiple tasks being run all relate to each other, and hence there is a strong interdependency. There is need for intertask communication and a question of priorities as to who gets control of the CPU and when. In multitasking such issues are determined by the operating system, while in multiprogramming this is left to the user. With multiprogramming operating systems on a microcomputer, the user can run and view many programs at the same time. A simple example of multiprogramming is the user running a spreadsheet program (for example, Lotus 1-2-3) on one window and word processing on another window. A simple example of multitasking is a user running a program consisting of two tasks: the first task is to read and display a temperature on the screen every second and the second task is to execute a control algorithm every tenth of a second. It is the function of RTOS to handle the occurrence of such multiple tasks, each contending for the CPU.

Real-time operating systems are much more complex than regular operating systems and hence not as readily available on microcomputers. It is only recently that a number of companies have announced software for microcomputers in this area.

Many DAC systems do not need the features of an RTOS. If the tasks to be accomplished by the system can be set up as a single program sequence, then a regular operating system is sufficient. On the other hand, if the tasks to be accomplished are many and may make simultaneous contention for control of the CPU, then an RTOS is required. Other areas where an RTOS is useful are

> to execute tasks on a timed basis
>
> to tie the execution of tasks to external events
>
> to assign priorities to tasks
>
> to execute tasks conditionally
>
> for intertask communication

We conclude this section with an example that illustrates the application of real-time programming.

Example   Climate Control of a Building

> Climate control of large buildings can be made more energy efficient by automatic control using microcomputers. The tasks involved here are
>
> > monitoring the temperature and humidity in each zone in the building and scheduling the flow of air
> >
> > anticipating heating or cooling from temperature forecasts and starting up appropriate cooling or heating units to meet scheduled needs
> >
> > monitoring fire alarms and activating appropriate water sprinklers in an emergency
> >
> > monitoring the status of heating and cooling units
> >
> > providing daily log summaries
> >
> > providing operators with current information
>
> Each of these tasks can be assigned a priority that will determine when the task will get control of the CPU. Further, the user will have to decide how often each task must be executed and what conditions will activate a task. Multitasking, real-time operating systems will simplify the job of programming complex DAC applications such as the above.

7.2 MULTITASKING

The concept of multitasking can be best illustrated using an example. Consider a process plant that is used to dry food in a drying oven. The following are the requirements of the proposed DAC system.

1. Monitor process variables such as temperature and humidity of air entering and leaving the process, the moisture content and temperature of the solids, the solids processing rate, and so on (every second).
2. Adjust the heating rate and air flow rate based on a predetermined formula (every second).
3. Display the process status on the screen (updated every 10 sec).
4. Print out a report every 4 hours summarizing the process operation.

We can think of setting up three logically separate program segments to accomplish each of the four objectives set forth above. We can describe these as three tasks:

Task 1: Monitor and control.

Task 2: Update display.

Task 3: Print report.

Each task can also be assigned a priority. In this example task 1 has highest priority, followed by task 2 and then task 3. The time taken to execute each task is different. Let us consider the following execution times.

Task 1: 0.5 sec

Task 2: 1.5 sec

Task 3: 10 sec

This implies that at the end of a 10-sec period, both task 1 and task 2 will be requesting control of the CPU. It is the job of the operating system to assign the control of the CPU to the highest-priority task. We will discuss this later.

For the moment, let us say that task 1 gets control of the CPU and runs to completion. At time = 10.5 sec, task 2 can start to execute, but it will not run to completion because task 1 gets active again at time = 11 sec. Thus task 2 has to be interrupted in the middle and its execution status saved, so that execution can resume precisely at the point where it was stopped. After task 1 is finished again task 2 can get control of the CPU and resume its execution. This process is repeated until task 2 is completed.

A similar set of events will take place when task 3 gets activated (that is, is ready for execution). This happens at time = 4 hours. But since this is a fairly long task, it will get interrupted again and again by the other two tasks.

Figure 7.1 illustrates graphically the events that take place in the execution of this "multitask program." Tasks can be programmed in a high-level language such as FOR-

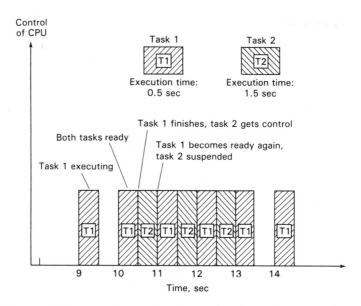

Figure 7.1 Illustrating the execution of two recurring tasks of different priorities

TRAN or BASIC. The extensions to the high-level languages that permit real-time programming are discussed in more detail later. But first we need to talk about some of the demands placed on the operating system.

7.3 REAL-TIME OPERATING SYSTEMS

So far we have covered three types of operating systems:

1. single-task operating systems
2. multiprogramming systems
3. multitask operating systems (also called real-time operating systems)

To accomplish data acquisition and control functions such as the one described above we need a multitasking operating system. Specifically, we need the ability to

1. Assign priorities to tasks.
2. Schedule tasks according to their priorities.
3. Suspend, kill, rejuvenate, and restart tasks.
4. Allow tasks to share data and send messages to one another.
5. Maintain a queue of active tasks.

All tasks that need to be executed are loaded into memory where they reside. A real-time operating system is usually implemented by setting up a queue of active tasks and then checking the queue at fixed intervals of time (for example, every 10 msec) to see which task should be given control of the CPU. A task can be in one of the following states:

1. *Executing:* This means that the task has control of the CPU.
2. *Ready:* This means that the task is waiting for availability of the CPU.
3. *Suspended:* This refers to a task that is waiting for some event to happen, such as a certain elapsed time to pass.
4. *Inactive:* This is a task that has completed execution and is no longer required.

Task Control

Tasks may be activated by commands from within other tasks. This is accomplished using a set of real-time commands that are part of the programming language. It includes commands to achieve the following:

1. Activate task, that is, put the task into a ready state.
2. Kill a task. Puts a task into an inactive state.
3. Suspend a task. This task may later be activated again.
4. Suspend execution of a task for a given period of time.
5. Activate a task at a given point in time.
6. Send and receive messages to and from another task.

These commands are usually integrated into higher-level programming languages supported by the RTOS.

Other Features to Look for in an RTOS

The variety of languages supported by the RTOS is an important criterion in the selection of the RTOS. For engineering applications, support of BASIC and FORTRAN should be required. Compatibility with the other common operating systems is another important consideration. The RTOS should use commands similar to the standard operating system. Disk files created in the multitask version of the operating system should be compatible with disk files created in the standard operating system.

Foreground/Background Operation

Some operating systems offer a simplified version of multitasking called *foreground/background* operation. This term is used to indicate the ability to run two programs simultaneously. The higher-priority task resides in the background and is executed at regular intervals of time. Whenever the CPU is free, the foreground program is given control. This may be viewed as a subset of a full-featured multitasking operating system. There are a number of companies that offer software for DAC with this feature. They operate under the normal operating system and use a feature of the CPU called the *interrupt line* to activate the background task. Interrupts are discussed in more detail in the next section.

7.4 INTERRUPTS

Consider a real-time application involving three tasks related to a reactor:

Task 1: Highest priority. Read temperature and check for high-limit violation of temperature. If temperature exceeds limit, immediately execute the code to shut down the reactor.

Task 2: Keep a log of temperature, one reading every second. Display the temperature on the screen.

Task 3: Every minute generate a printout of the temperature log.

Since task 1 has highest priority it must be executed as often as possible. If we execute it too often, then task 2 may not get control of the CPU at all and the system will have failed to meet its objectives. Thus we have a problem.

Problems of this type can be solved using the interrupt capability of the CPU. Most CPUs have a dedicated line called the interrupt line. External devices can get the attention of the CPU by activating this line. The way the interrupt is handled is dependent on the operating system. In the case of the Apple II computer, an interrupt will cause the CPU to halt execution of the current program and cause an execution of a program stored at a specific location in memory.

Some real-time operating systems allow many devices to interrupt the CPU. In this case, after an interrupt is detected, the device causing the interrupt must be identified. It can be done in software (by asking each device to identify whether it caused the interrupt) or in hardware (this is called the *vectored* interrupt feature).

Using the interrupt feature, the output of the temperature sensor can be used to activate one of the interrupt lines and we can program the computer to activate task 1 whenever this interrupt occurs. This avoids the need to constantly check the temperature for limit violation, and leaves the CPU free to do the other tasks. Interrupt handling is available on some (not all) real-time operating systems.

7.5 REAL-TIME PROGRAMMING LANGUAGES

Real-time programming languages are usually extensions of the popular programming languages. Thus we have

real-time BASIC
real-time FORTRAN
ADA
C
PASCAL

Of these only ADA has any standards specified for these real-time extensions. The Instrument Society of America (ISA) has proposed some standards for real-time extensions to FORTRAN, but they do not cover all the features, and it remains to be seen if this will become an industrywide standard.

The real-time extensions consist of the following functional groups:

1. executive interface routines
2. process input/output routines
3. file handling subroutines
4. task management routines

Executive Interface Routines

These are subroutine calls from the high-level language to the operating system to control task execution. Some examples are

1. Start a task at a specified time of day.
2. Start a task after a specified elapsed time.
3. Assign a priority to a task.
4. Obtain the time of day.
5. Lock and unlock access to devices.
6. Schedule a task on a cyclical basis (repeated execution).

Process Input/Output

These are subroutine calls to acquire data from process input interfaces and to send data to process output interfaces. Some examples are

1. Read an analog input channel.
2. Send a signal to an analog output channel.
3. Read a digital input word.

File Handling

These routines allow creating and opening a disk file, reading and writing data to the disk file, and closing the file. These features are also covered in languages such as

FORTRAN-77. One problem that is important in real-time operation is the conflict that might arise when two tasks use the same file.

Task Management Routines

These include routines for suspending a task, killing a task (meaning that the task is no longer needed), activating a task when an event happens (for example, when an interrupt occurs), delaying execution of a task for a specified period of time, and so on.

SUMMARY

Many DAC applications can be programmed using a single-task operating system. Occasionally the need arises for breaking the software into tasks, assigning task priorities, and controlling the timed execution of these tasks. Such situations call for the use of a multitasking, real-time operating system. The RTOS will handle the queueing and execution of tasks according to their priorities. RTOS will generally support high-level languages such as FORTRAN and BASIC. Each task then is coded like a subroutine. Some attempts have been made to standardize real-time languages.

Interrupts are a convenient way of detecting external events such as the closure of a switch. Using the interrupt capability, one can free the computer from having to constantly check whether the external event has occurred. Some operating systems support interrupt handling. Interrupt inputs are treated differently from digital inputs.

REVIEW QUESTIONS

1. The human brain is a wonderful example of a multitasking operating system. List and elaborate on the tasks involved in driving a car from home to work, or alternatively, in preparing for an exam or playing a particular sport.

2. Consider the problem of designing a computer to automate the machine used to fill bottles with liquid. The machine fills a moving assembly line of bottles one by one. Each bottle must be filled with a predetermined amount of liquid. The assembly line can be started and stopped by the computer. In addition to filling the bottles, the computer should provide an operator interface for display of data and to accept new commands. List all the tasks involved. Which task has the highest priority? Should one use interrupt-driven software?

3. What is meant by the following terms:
   (a) task priority
   (b) kill a task
   (c) suspend a task
   (d) ready a task
   (e) task queue

4. What are the important features that distinguish a real-time operating system from a non-real-time operating system?

5. How is multitasking different from multiprogramming?

6. Consider the problem of scheduling the arrival and departure of trains at a train station.
   (a) List various tasks involved and assign priorities.
   (b) Outline the sequence of events that take place when a train arrives at the station.

REFERENCES

MELLICHAMP, D. A., ED. *Real-Time Computing with Applications to Data Acquisition and Control.* New York: Van Nostrand Reinhold, 1983.
This book is a compendium on all topics related to real-time computing. It contains chapters on RTOS, real-time FORTRAN, and real-time BASIC.

FOSTER, C. C. *Real-Time Programming: Neglected Topics.* Reading, MA: Addison-Wesley, 1982.
This makes interesting reading and contains many illustrative programs in assembly language. Recommended for those who want to learn more about the hardware and software related to real-time computers.

SAVITSKY, S. R. *Real-Time Microprocessor Systems.* New York: Van Nostrand Reinhold, 1985.

LIST OF SOFTWARE VENDORS

The following is a partial listing of companies that market RTOS software. Complete addresses can be found in Appendix B.

Action Instruments
Analog Devices
Data General Corp.
Digital Equipment Corp.
Hewlett-Packard
Intel
Microway
Motorola Semiconductor Products, Inc.

8

Control Using
the Computer

8.1 Introduction

One of the advantages of replacing conventional analog data recording and control instruments with a microcomputer is the ability to implement more intelligent and flexible controllers on the microcomputer. Significant improvement in the system performance can be achieved by better control of process variables. In this chapter, we will discuss basic concepts of feedback control and how these can be implemented using a microcomputer.

The majority of control systems use a feedback of some measurement on the process to activate the control mechanism. Figure 8.1 shows an example of a conventional feedback control system. The control objective in this example is to maintain the temperature in the tank at a desired value by controlling the steam flow into the heating coil inside the tank. The major components of the feedback loop are further exemplified in the block diagram shown in Figure 8.2. The variable to be controlled is measured and the signal from the measurement sensor is sent to the controller. The controller compares the measured value against the desired value (called the *set point* of the controlled output variable) and decides on the control action to be taken. This control signal is then transmitted back to the actuator on the process. This completes the feedback loop. The output variable may deviate from the set point either because the set point is changed deliberately by the operator or because of external disturbances entering the process.

In computer control, we want to replace the controller shown in Figures 8.1 and 8.2 with the computer. The output to be sent to the actuator will then be determined by the control logic programmed within the computer.

Figure 8.3 shows the block diagram of the same control system with the controller replaced by a computer. In this case the measurement is sent to the computer via an input

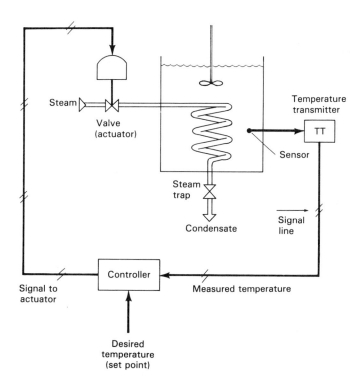

Figure 8.1   Feedback control of temperature in a stirred tank

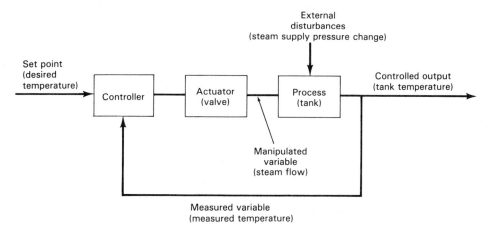

Figure 8.2   Block diagram of feedback control system

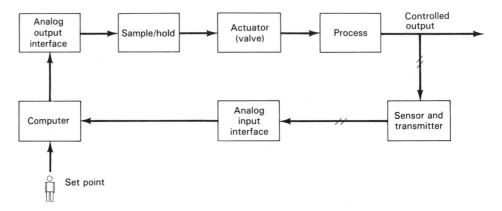

Figure 8.3   Computer control of temperature

interface (either analog or digital). Similarly, the output to the actuator is sent via an output interface. We have shown a sample and hold block in both input and output interface to emphasize the fact that the computer is reading and outputting only at discrete points in time whereas the process operates continuously.

This chapter is concerned with the design of computer control systems such as the one shown in Figure 8.3. We begin by first discussing the methodology of conventional analog control. Most of this technology carries over to the digital control system design. This is followed by a discussion of advanced control strategies. Some commercially available hardware and software for process control is discussed in the last section.

8.2 ANALOG CONTROL TECHNIQUES

The controller's function is to determine what action to take based on the measurement it receives from the process. The logic used in analog controllers is necessarily simple because of the difficulty of building complex logic in analog circuits. We will focus our attention on the single input/single output (SISO) system, that is, control of a single output using a single manipulated variable. The logic used in this case in analog controllers has proved to be very effective and in fact is adapted in computer control as well.

Analog controllers can be either *pneumatic* or *electronic*. Pneumatic controllers operate using air pressure to indicate and transmit signals. These were popular up until the 1960s. These are still in use today in some instances where use of electricity may be hazardous. Pneumatic controllers use a 20-psig (pounds per square inch gauge) air supply for power and use 3–15 psi air pressure lines for signal transmission. Electronic controllers operate using 4 to 20 mA for signal transmission. Current is preferred over voltage because of noise immunity and ability to transmit over longer distances. In a plant, the controllers are situated in a central room physically separated from the rest of the plant. Controllers are rack mounted and put on display panels for easy access by plant operators.

There are primarily four major types of controllers that are used in SISO feedback control. These are *on/off, proportional (P), proportional-integral (PI)*, and *proportional-integral-derivative (PID)* controllers. These are discussed one by one below.

On/Off Control

This is the simplest type of single-loop feedback control. The logic can be explained with respect to the tank temperature control example of Figure 8.1. The controller turns the steam valve full open if tank temperature is below the set point and the steam valve is turned off if the temperature is above the set point.

On/off control generally leads to imperfect control. Figure 8.4 shows the typical temperature behavior.

Note that the temperature of the tank keeps on rising even after the steam valve is shut off. This is due to the inherent capacities of the process. The temperature keeps rising until all the steam in the line is condensed. Likewise when the valve is turned on, it takes some time for the steam to fill the coil and heat the coil. The temperature will rise only after the coil has heated up.

This cyclic behavior can get worse if the capacities of the system increase. Because

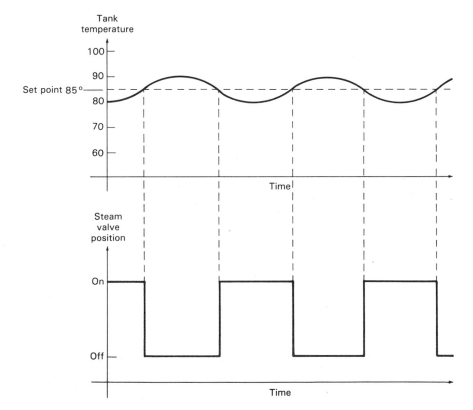

Figure 8.4   Typical tank temperature behavior under on/off control

of this inherent behavior, on/off control is not used in applications where precise control is necessary.

The main advantage of on/off control is the simplicity of the controller and the actuator. On/off control is used in many household appliances to control temperature (water heater, oven, electric iron, and so on). The thermostats used in room temperature control also employ on/off control.

Most on/off controllers are built with a certain dead zone, that is, a region of measured variable in which no action is taken. Thus, in the above example, if the temperature lies within, say, 5° of the set point, no action is taken. This prevents the valve from being turned on/off continuously due to noise present in the measurement. The presence of the dead zone increases the oscillations that arise in the temperature.

Proportional (P) Control

Proportional controllers vary the manipulated variable continuously to achieve better control. The actuator used in proportional control must be able to vary the manipulated variable (for example, steam flow) continuously over a range from completely on to off.

The corrective action taken by the controller is proportional to the error in the controlled variable. For the temperature control example the signal to the control valve is computed as follows. Let

$$T_{\text{set}} = \text{set point of temperature}$$

$$T_m = \text{measure temperature}$$

Then

$$e = T_{\text{set}} - T_m$$

$$\Delta m = K_c \cdot e$$

where K_c is a constant of proportionately called *controller gain*. Δm is the change in signal to the steam valve computed by the controller. In reality the controller computes

$$m = m_s + \Delta m$$

where m_s is a nominal value. The value m is sent to the control valve (for example, 4 mA current to close valve, 20 mA current to open valve).

The value of m_s is selected by the user. Note that when the error is zero the controller output will be equal to m_s. Hence m_s can be thought of as the steady state controller output when there are no disturbances in the system. This value is set when the controller is turned on and remains constant until the controller is turned off.

Tuning the controller involves selecting an appropriate value for the controller gain. Small values of K_c lead to sluggish responses (corrective action taken is small) and larger values lead to faster responses. As K_c becomes very large, this controller behaves like an on/off controller, since even small errors will cause the valve to go fully on to fully off. In this case, oscillations will result. In practice a value of K_c must be selected to yield optimum performance.

Another problem that arises with proportional controllers is that they do not always reduce the error in the controlled variable to zero. Consider the tank temperature control. If for some reason the ambient temperature were to drop and heat losses from the tank were to increase, this would require an increase in the nominal steam supply. This can only be accomplished by maintaining a positive error, and hence the temperature will never quite equal the set point until the ambient temperature returns to its nominal value. This nominal error in the controlled variable is called the steady state *offset*. Offsets can be eliminated using PI controllers, described next.

Proportional-Integral (PI) Control

This controller avoids the problem of steady state offset by using the total error accumulating in time ($\int edt$) in the control action. The equation for the PI controller is

$$m = K_c e + \frac{K_c}{T_I} \int edt$$

The first term is identical to the control law used with the proportional controller. The second term, weighted by the factor $\frac{1}{T_I}$, is called the *integral term*. T_I is called the *integral time constant*. As error accumulates in time, this term becomes more significant. Eventually the error is driven to zero by this term.

Note that the term m_s is absent in the PI control equation. The reason is that the integral term will approach a value necessary to drive this error to zero. Thus even when the error goes to zero, the controller output will be a nonzero value determined by the integral term.

Tuning a proportional controller requires choosing the appropriate values of K_c and T_I to yield optimum performance.

Integral action brings with it two problems. First, it slows down the control action slightly. Second, if the process is out of control for a sufficiently long period of time, the integral term can accumulate and saturate. This is called *reset windup*. In this case it will take some time before the controller is brought back to normal operation. Conventional control systems are built to contain sufficient safeguards to prevent saturation in case of control failure. This must be kept in mind in digital implementations as well.

Proportional-Integral-Derivative (PID) Control

The control equation for the PID controller is given by

$$m = K_c e = \frac{K_c}{T_I} \int edt + K_c T_D \frac{de}{dt}$$

The derivative term anticipates the direction of change of the error and hence speeds up the control action. Tuning this controller requires finding the optimum values of the three variables K_c, T_I, and T_D. Derivative action is used on slow responding processes. Reset windup can be a problem with this controller also.

Controller Faceplates

The above controllers are rack mounted in a control panel. The faceplates (an example of which is shown in Figure 8.5) show the measured variable, the set point, and the controller output. In addition, the auto/manual switch enables the operator to set the controller output directly if this is desirable. A set point adjustment allows the operator to change the set point. If the set point can be set remotely through another signal line, then a local/remote switch is also provided.

Controller tuning knobs for K_c, T_I, and T_D are provided on the side of the controller.

Controller Tuning

Standard procedures have been established for tuning the controller to achieve optimum performance. Optimum performance, however, is a subjective criterion. Generally two types of tests are used.

The first is called *set point response method*. In this case, a step increase is made in

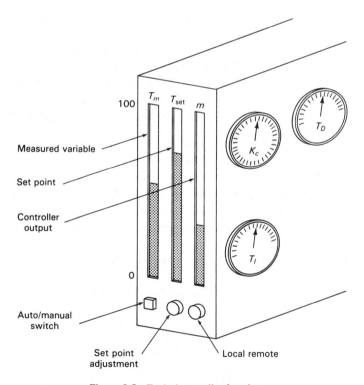

Figure 8.5 Typical controller faceplate

the set point while the controller is on automatic (feedback loop closed) and the response of the controlled output is recorded. Figure 8.6 illustrates a typical response. Ideally the new set point would be attained instantaneously. In practice an attempt is made to minimize the shaded area. Other measures are the overshoot (see Figure 8.6) and the time taken to settle within 99% of the new set point.

The second test that is used to check controller performance is based on applying a load (disturbance) to the process and observing how well the controller performs in bringing the output back to its set point. Again a typical response is shown in Figure 8.6. The objective is to minimize the shaded area, which is one measure of the quality of control.

There are a number of ways to tune the controller. Two methods are described here. The first is based on an open-loop response of the process and is called the *Ziegler-Nichols reaction curve method*. The reaction curve is obtained by putting the controller on manual and then making a step increase in the controller output. This will cause the process output to change and settle to a new value. Most systems show a response similar to the one

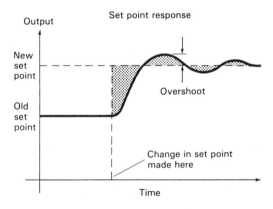

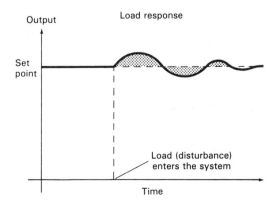

Figure 8.6 Controller tuning

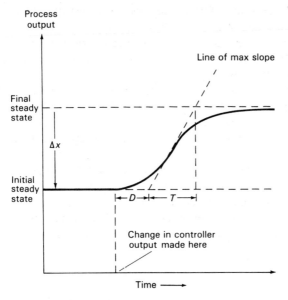

Process gain $K_P = \dfrac{\Delta x}{\Delta m}$

Change in controller output = Δm

Figure 8.7 Open-loop (manual control) response to a step increase in controller output showing how K_p, T, and D are completed

depicted in Figure 8.7. This is used to identify the parameters K_p, T, and D of the system as shown in the figure.

Based on the parameters K_p, T, and D identified in Figure 8.7, the controller parameters proposed by Ziegler and Nichols are shown in Table 8.1. These are suggested only as starting points for further fine tuning of the controller.

Not all processes may exhibit the response type shown in Figure 8.7. If the process response varies significantly, then this tuning method will not be applicable.

Another approach to estimating the controller tuning parameters is based on the controller gain (under proportional control only), which causes the system to continuously oscillate without settling down. This gain is called the *ultimate gain,* and the period that the output oscillates is called the *ultimate period.* Any gain greater than this ultimate gain will cause the oscillations to increase in amplitude with time and the process will go unstable. The controller constants suggested by Ziegler and Nichols, based on the ultimate gain K_u and the ultimate period P_u, are shown in Table 8.2. As in the previous method,

TABLE 8.1 CONTROLLER TUNING BY ZIEGLER-NICHOLS REACTION CURVE METHOD

Controller constant	P only	PI	PID
Gain K_c	$T/(K_p D)$	$0.9T/(K_p D)$	$1.2T/(K_p D)$
Integral time T_I		$D/0.3$	$D/0.5$
Derivative time T_D			$0.5D$

TABLE 8.2 CONTROLLER TUNING USING
ZIEGLER-NICHOLS ULTIMATE GAIN METHOD

Controller constant	P only	PI	PID
Gain K_c	$Ku/2$	$Ku/2.2$	$Ku/1.7$
Integral time T_I		$Pu/1.2$	$Pu/1.2$
Derivative time T_D			$Pu/8$

the values suggested in this table should be used as starting points for further fine tuning of the controller.

8.3 DIGITAL IMPLEMENTATON

Now we turn our attention to the realization of the above types of controllers using a computer. The digital implementation of each of the four types of controllers are as follows.

This is the program logic required for computer implementation of on/off control:

Step 1   Read analog input channel to obtain measurement of controlled output T_m.

Step 2   If $|T_m - T_{set}| < = \epsilon$, do nothing. Here ϵ represents the dead zone, in which no control action is taken.

Step 3   If $T_m > T_{set} + \epsilon$, turn off manipulated variable by outputting a 0 on the digital output channel corresponding to the actuator.

Step 4   If $T_m < T_{set} - \epsilon$, turn on manipulated variable by outputting a 1 on the digital output channel.

Step 5   Return to step 1 or return to calling program.

The parameters T_{set} and ϵ must be specified by the user in appropriate units. In addition, the program also needs the address of the analog input channel and the digital output channel.

The frequency at which the user wants to update the control action will determine the frequency of execution of this program. It is recommended that the controller output be updated at a frequency at least 10 times greater than the frequency of oscillation observed for the output under analog on/off control (see Figure 8.4). At high frequencies of updating the performance of the digital implementation will approach that of the analog controller.

Proportional Control

The program logic required to implement proportional control is as follows:

1. Read the analog channel connected to the output to be controlled.

2. Check the value read for limit violation; do noise filtering if necessary. If the value read is outside the limits, print message to operator (possible sensor failure) and return to calling program.
3. Compute the error ($e = T_{set} - T_m$).
4. Compute the controller output: $m = m_s + K_c e$.
5. Check m for limit violations. If m exceeds the maximum, set it equal to the max. If m is below the minimum, set it equal to the min.
6. Send m to the analog output channel connected to the manipulated variable.
7. Return to calling program.

This program requires the following parameters:

T_{set}:   set point controlled variable
T_{max}:   maximum possible value of measured variable
T_{min}:   minimum possible value of measured variable
K_c: controller gain
m_s: controller output when error e is zero
m_{min}:   minimum value of controller output
m_{max}:   maximum value of controller output

In addition, the addresses of analog input and analog output channels that are used to interface to the process are required.

The value of K_c is determined by controller tuning. Provisions must be made for the operator to be able to change T_{set} during program execution. m_s is best determined from a plot of T versus m under steady state conditions and using manual mode of operation.

Note that due to the discrete nature of digital implementation, control action is taken only at discrete points in time. This discrete nature of digital control introduces an additional delay in the feedback control loop. Too large a sampling time (time interval between control activities) can cause the control quality to degrade.

There are two alternate ways to send the output to the actuator. These are as follows:

Position form: $m_n = m_s + K_c e_n$
Velocity form: $m_n = m_{n-1} + K_c(e_n - e_{n-1})$

Here m_n is the new controller output and m_{n-1} is the controller output from the previous execution of the control subprogram.

In the velocity form, m_s is not required. Only the change in m is computed and implemented. This has the advantage of bumpless transfer (no sudden change in m) when the controller is switched from manual to automatic.

Proportional Integral Control

Integral action is computed using the approximation

$$\int_0^t edt = \sum_{n=0}^{N} e_n \Delta t$$

where Δt is the sampling time, e_n is the error at the nth sample, and N is the total number of samples in the interval 0 to t. In actual implementation, this integral is stored by using a variable s, as follows:

$$s_n = s_{n-1} + e_n \Delta t$$

where e_n is the current error and s_n is the integral term.

When using the velocity form this can also be avoided:

$$m_n = m_{n-1} + K_c (e_n - e_{n-1}) + \frac{K_c}{T_I} (e_n) \Delta t$$

There is no need to store all past values of e_i and m_i in computer memory; only the current value and the value at the previous sampling time are required.

This controller requires knowledge of sampling time and assumes that the sampling time is constant. This should be kept in mind during the implementation. One strategy is to execute this program at predetermined intervals of time.

Reset windup problems can appear here, too. Integration should be stopped if the controller is on manual. Also, upper and lower limits should be set on the contribution of the integral term.

PID Control

Recall that the derivative term is computed as de/dt. In digital implementation this can be calculated as

$$\frac{de}{dt} \approx \frac{e_n - e_{n-1}}{\Delta t}$$

It should be noted that this is an approximation and is very sensitive to noise in the computed error values. Hence derivative action should not be used with measurements that are noise prone. Keeping Δt small can amplify this problem, since Δt appears in the denominator.

Sampling Time

One feature introduced in the digital implementation of analog control equations is the sampling of measured variables. As mentioned earlier, this acts like a delay in the measurements and hence causes the controller performance to degrade. It is recommended that this sampling time be kept smaller than $\frac{1}{10}$ of the time constant of the process (given by T in Figure 8.7).

The tuning of digital controllers above can be done in a manner identical to that of the analog controllers. Since there are no knobs to adjust, provisions should be made for the operator to enter the tuning parameters through the keyboard.

8.4 ADVANCED CONTROL

Feedforward Control

Feedforward control is based on the concept of anticipating the effect of disturbances on the output and then taking control actions that nullify the effect of these disturbances. Figure 8.8 shows the strategy of feedforward control.

The simpler types of feedforward control involve a proportional-type control action based on the variation in the disturbance variable:

$$m = K_c d$$

where

m = manipulated input

d = measured disturbance

and K_c is adjusted to yield good steady state compensation. Some improvement is obtainable by incorporating a time-dependent form in the control law. Interested readers are referred to the books on process control cited at the end of this chapter.

Usually feedforward action is combined with feedback, since it is impossible to measure and compensate for all disturbances and because of the errors introduced by improper feedforward compensation.

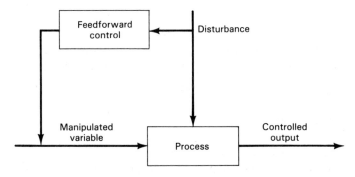

Figure 8.8   Feedforward control strategy

Cascade Control

Cascade control utilizes multiple control loops to achieve better immunity to input disturbances. Consider the temperature control system of Figure 8.1 again. If for some reason
the steam pressure were to change, this would cause a decrease in the steam flow and
condensation temperature. This would then affect the heat transferred, which would
ultimately affect the tank temperature. The temperature controller will then bring the
steam flow under control. While this is adequate, control quality will be poor because of
all the time lags involved between the steam pressure change and tank temperature.

An alternative to this is cascade control structure, shown in Figure 8.9. This structure consists of two loops. The inner loop controls the flow of steam. A flow transmitter
(FT) senses and transmits the flow. The flow controller (FC) adjusts the valve position to
maintain steam flow equal to the set point. The set point is supplied by the temperature
controller (TC). This way any disturbances in steam pressure are canceled by the actions
of the flow controller.

Cascade loops are suggested when the inner loop can respond faster than the outer
loop to cancel out the effect of disturbances. However, if the inner loop is slow in
reacting, the benefits of cascade control will not be achieved.

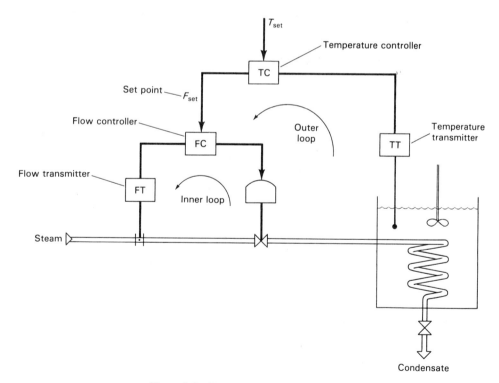

Figure 8.9 Cascade control of tank temperature

A word of caution here is that if the inner loop is put on manual, then the outer loop should also automatically go to manual. Otherwise, reset windup will occur in the outer loop.

8.5 INTEGRATED HARDWARE AND SOFTWARE FOR CONTROL

Instead of developing the hardware and software components necessary for a DAC system, the user can solve the problem by

1. purchasing integrated software from third-party vendors that will allow easy integration of the data gathering and control tasks
2. purchasing an integrated hardware plus software system built specifically for DAC applications

The latter, commonly referred to as a *distributed control system,* is generally sold by instrumentation and control companies such as Honeywell, Foxboro, Fisher, and Taylor. The former category is a low-cost alternative for small applications involving fewer than 100 data acquisition points and one or two dozen control loops. Each category is discussed in some detail below.

Integrated Software Packages

These packages are intended to relieve the user of the burden of developing, coding, and testing software for DAC applications. The idea is to anticipate the most common requirements of DAC software and then to provide these functions with easy-to-use, menu-driven formats. The functions most commonly needed are

data logging at specified intervals
display of data in tabular and graphical form
configuration of control loops using common control algorithms
trend display (that is, display of historical trends in process variables)
alarm setting/monitoring
redundancy in the form of alternative hardware backup systems
process diagnosis/monitoring
report generation
user-programmed control function
graphical display of process and control-loop configuration

Not all functions may be available with any one package. The software is sold for specific computer systems and may support a variety of hardware interfaces. Costs range from under $1000 for simple systems to $30,000 or more for complex packages. Some manufacturers are listed at the end of this chapter.

Some key questions to ask when evaluating these packages are

1. How easy is it to set up a DAC system using this software?
2. Does it provide the critical functions you need?
3. What kinds of controllers does it provide?
4. Is it possible to add new functions to the system?
5. What is the maximum number of points it can monitor? What is the maximum number of control loops?
6. What is its capacity for future expansion?
7. Does it have self-tuning controllers?
8. What kind of redundancy does it support?
9. In the event of computer failure, will data be lost? Will the process go out of control?
10. Does the software check for hardware failure? If so, what does it do?

Distributed Control Systems

As mentioned earlier, these are integrated hardware plus software packages offered by control instrumentation manufacturers. The architecture of distributed control systems is shown in Figure 8.10. The key component here is a network databus—often called the *data highway*—through which all communications take place. Various types of digital devices can be attached to the highway. These include

controller modules (microprocessor-based controllers)

programmable logic controllers (for control of discrete event systems)

operator consoles for display of process information

manager consoles

host minicomputer

communication hardware

permanent storage devices

The modular structure allows it to expand as needs increase. The use of multiple microprocessor systems provides for redundancy to cope with component failures. These systems are expensive, with prices starting at around $50,000.

With the current popularity of microcomputers, many of the manufacturers are providing the capability to access the network from a microcomputer. This would be particularly helpful for plant engineers or managers who want to access the plant data and process it on their microcomputers.

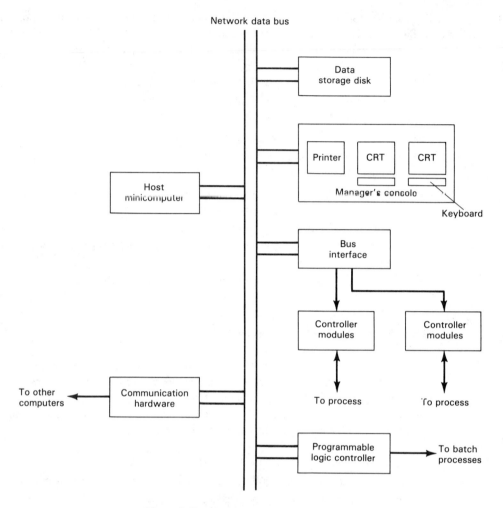

Figure 8.10   Distributed control system structure

SUMMARY

This chapter provided a brief look at the methodology commonly employed in control of systems. The four basic types of controllers (on/off, proportional, proportional-integral, and proportional-integral-derivative) account for the majority of control loops employed in industry. The digital implementation of these controllers was discussed. Controller parameters are set by various controller tuning methods, two of which were discussed in this chapter. Finally, for those who do not want to invest heavily in developing their own software, prepackaged software exists that allows configuration and implementation of control systems using a microcomputer. Another more expensive alternative here involves integrated hardware plus software packages offered by control instrumentation vendors.

REVIEW QUESTIONS

1. How does one choose between on/off, proportional, proportional-integral, and proportional-integral-derivative controllers?

2. How does one choose a sampling frequency for feedback control applications? What effect does increasing the sampling frequency have on the controller performance?

3. What is meant by tuning a controller? How does one tune a PID controller?

4. Survey the market for control software for your microcomputer. Are there some that can meet your DAC needs?

5. What is meant by a distributed control system? What is a programmable controller?

6. List the pros and cons of using a distributed control system versus a microcomputer-based control system.

7. What is a data highway?

8. What is meant by redundancy in a control system? How can redundancy be achieved?

9. What is meant by a cascade control system? List possible areas where cascade control might be used.

REFERENCES

There are a number of good books on control. A few of them are listed below.

ASTROM, K. J., AND B. WITTENMARK. *Computer Controlled Systems.* Englewood Cliffs, NJ: Prentice-Hall, 1984.

DESHPANDE, P. *Elements of Computer Control with Advanced Control Applications.* Research Triangle Park, NC: Instrument Society of America, 1984.

FRANKLIN, G. F., AND J. D. POWELL. *Digital Control of Dynamic Systems.* Reading, PA: Addison-Wesley, 1981.

HARRISON, T. J., ED. *Minicomputers in Industrial Control.* Research Triangle Park, NC: Instrument Society of America, 1978.

KUO, B. C. *Digital Control Systems.* Champaign, IL: SRL Publishing Co., 1977.

PATRICK, D. R., AND S. W. FARDO. *Industrial Process Control Systems.* Indianapolis, IN: Sams, 1979.

SMITH, C. A., AND A. B. CORRIPIO. *Principles and Practice of Automatic Process Control.* New York: Wiley, 1985.

The following two books discuss integrated hardware and software for process control.

LUKAS, M. P. *Distributed Control Systems: Their Evaluation and Design.* New York: Van Nostrand Reinhold, 1986.

MOORE, J. A., AND S. M. HERB. *Understanding Distributed Process Control.* Research Triangle Park, NC: Instrument Society of America, 1983.

The book by Mellichamp listed in Chapters 2, 5, and 7 also contains some excellent chapters on various aspects of control using minicomputers.

LIST OF MANUFACTURERS

The following is a partial list of companies that provide hardware and software for process control using microcomputers. Complete addresses can be found in Appendix B.

Analog Devices
Centec Corp.
Controlsoft, Inc.
Data Acquisition Systems
Digital Equipment Corp.
Equinox Data Corp.
Gerry Engineering Software
Heuristics, Inc.
Loyola Controls, Inc.
Motorola Semiconductor Products, Inc.
Rogers Labs
Taylor Industrial Software

9

Data Management
and Analysis Software

9.1 DATA MANAGEMENT AND ANALYSIS REQUIREMENTS

In the area of data management and analysis, the microcomputer offers significant opportunities for productivity improvements. The purpose of this chapter is to examine the tools available on a microcomputer to enhance and facilitate the data management and analysis functions.

We concentrate our attention primarily on data handling requirements in a laboratory or pilot plant environment. The requirements in such environments tend to be more diverse than in production plant environments.

First, let us consider the information handling requirements of DAC systems. These requirements will provide the background for examining available software tools. We can divide the requirements into the following categories:

1. data analysis
2. data archival and retrieval
3. data display and reporting

Typical data analysis requirements include

conversion of acquired data to engineering units
filtering the noise in the measurements
frequency content analysis
input data checking

statistical analysis such as computation of mean, variance, standard deviation, and so on

correlation of data to determine possible relationships among different data items

linear and nonlinear regression of data to obtain parameters in models

peak detection and integration for the analysis of chromatographic column data

Typical data management requirements include

ability to organize and store data from an experiment or plant

ability to retrieve the data in various formats

provide security of the data to prevent loss and/or use by unauthorized personnel

generate daily, weekly, or monthly reports from the data

combine data from different sources

sort the data according to user-specified criteria and categories

Finally, the data display and reporting requirements include the ability to

display and print acquired data in a variety of graphical forms, such as x-y plots, bar charts, pie charts, and 3-D graphs

prepare summary reports incorporating the results from the experiment or plant operation

In the following pages, we will look at some software tools for data handling on microcomputers. Many of these were developed in the context of data handling in a business environment, but they are equally applicable in the laboratory or plant.

9.2 DATABASE MANAGEMENT SYSTEMS (DBMS)

A DBMS is a software package designed to facilitate the handling of data. It has the following major components:

1. The database.   This is a collection of files containing all user-entered data. The user defines the organizational structure of the data without any reference to how the data is actually stored in the system. Various structures have been developed, but at present, the relational data structure seems to be winning out.

2. The database manager.   This component deals with storage of data in files on the disk, retrieval of an item, checking the data, security of data, time and date stamping of data files, and keeping a log of changes made to files.

3. A query language.   This is the input language for the user to interrogate the database for specific pieces of information.

4. Report generator.   This program allows the data to be extracted from the database and presented in the form of a report. The user can specify the data items to be included and their format.

5. Utilities.   This is to create new data files, enter data into existing files, sort data in files, create new files from existing data files, and interface to other software.

Example 1

An analytical laboratory does routine analysis of samples using a variety of instruments. Every sample brought to the lab must be identified with a number assigned by the lab. Table 9.1 shows the typical information that comes with each sample. Table 9.2 shows the result of one analysis entered into the database.

With a DBMS, the user first creates the structure of each table and defines the data type, column width, valid range, and so on for each column entry. The column headings also identify each variable.

During the data entry phase, the DBMS automatically sets up a menu-driven query sequence for the user to enter the data items. Figure 9.1 shows a typical query sequence. The input data is checked by the DBMS as it is entered.

TABLE 9.1   SAMPLE DATA

Sample no.	Date	Source	Ultimate analysis	Proximate analysis	Ash analysis	Moisture content
			Analysis required			
57825	1-10-86	ABC Co.	Yes	Yes	Yes	Yes
58241	1-11-86	CWRU	Yes	Yes	No	No
42126	1-11-86	Washington University	Yes	No	No	Yes
34221	1-12-86	XYZ Co.	Yes	Yes	No	No

TABLE 9.2   ULTIMATE ANALYSIS

Sample no.	Carbon	Hydrogen	Nitrogen	Oxygen	Date completed
57825	22	40	5	3	1-15-86
58241	21	42	4	2	1-16-86
42126	25	42	5	3	1-16-86

```
Sample no.          :
Date                :
Source              :
Ultimate analysis   :
Proximate analysis  :
Ash analysis        :
Moisture content    :
```

Figure 9.1   Typical query sequence for data entry

DBMS offers great flexibility in the retrieval of information. This is its advantage. For example, it is possible to ask questions such as

1. List all samples that arrived on January 10, 1986.
2. List all samples for which a proximate analysis needs to be performed.
3. List all samples with an ultimate analysis of hydrogen greater than 5%.
4. List all samples for XYZ Co. that arrived on January 10, 1986.

The file structure may be expanded as needs change. For example, if new analytical equipment is obtained, a column may be added to Table 9.1. Similarly, new relations (for example, list of addresses of companies, list of costs for each analysis, and so on) may be added to the database.

The report writing functions allow summary reports, including totals, averages, mean, and so forth, to be printed from the tables. Bills and invoices may also be prepared from the data files. Because many of the required functions are built in, the user is freed from the drudgery of programming.

DBMS for Microcomputers

DBMS was originally developed for large mainframe computers and used to cost in the hundreds of thousands of dollars. The arrival of the microcomputers fostered the development of smaller, easier-to-learn-and-use DBMS costing in the range of $100–$15,000. Emphasis on these systems is on serving the needs of individual users. As a result, these programs come with much improved documentation, on-line help facilities, menu-driven command structure, and instructional software. This approach has been so successful that manufacturers of large-scale DBMS have begun to provide compatible versions of their systems that run on microcomputers.

LIMS: Laboratory Information Management Systems

This is a new breed of DBMS that has been created specifically for managing data in research laboratories, quality control/quality assurance laboratories, and commercial testing laboratories. LIMS have been developed by the laboratory instrumentation companies and can be thought of as DBMS with a built-in data structure and data models tailored to meet the specific requirements in the laboratory. The advantage of a LIMS is that the user is relieved of the responsibility of designing and building the database structure. The disadvantages are that the LIMS are not as flexible as general-purpose DBMS are and may cost more.

Do You Need DBMS?

In addition to the purchase cost, the use of DBMS involves a certain amount of time and effort in learning to use the system. A careful evaluation of the data management needs must be made before plunging into this area. Some important questions to ask are

1. What kind of data is currently generated in the DAC application?
2. What kind of data analysis is needed? What might be desirable?
3. Is the data very volatile and short lived? In this case, DBMS might be of limited use.
4. What kind of security is required for the data? Can DBMS provide that security?
5. Does the data have to be accessed by multiple users simultaneously?
6. What are the report writing and forms generation requirements?
7. What is the size of the data to be handled? How will it be entered? Can the DBMS handle this volume of data?
8. How will the DBMS communicate with data produced by instruments and sensors?

A prototype of a database should first be created using simple examples to evaluate the feasibility of DBMS available on the market. Many manufacturers provide demonstration diskettes that illustrate the features of their software.

9.3 SPREADSHEET PROGRAMS

We now turn our attention to another productivity tool, *spreadsheet programs*, which have proved to be quite popular in the business environment. Many features of this type of software can be used in handling data associated with DAC systems as well.

What Can Spreadsheet Programs Do?

A spreadsheet is an expandable table of entries that are linked to each other through mathematically defined relations. Whenever one entry of the table is changed, the others linked to this entry are automatically updated. This is where the power of spreadsheets lies: in the ability to repeat calculations. Other useful features include the ability to print reports from portions of the table, draw graphs of various kinds, and do some minimal database operations.

Example 2

A laboratory is conducting test runs on a pilot plant. The data acquired and the data desired to be summarized for each run are shown in Table 9.3.

Note that some entries in the column are computed from the other entries using algebraic formulas. This must be repeated for each run.

In a spreadsheet program each location in the table is called a *cell*. Each cell is identified by the cell location; for example, B2 refers to the cell in which the unit of temperature T_2 is stored. Hence B2 contains the value K. Likewise cell C3 contains the value 115.0.

The relationship between cells that contain the mean temperature and the other cells is entered by the cell formula

$$C6 = \frac{C2 + C3 + C4 + C5}{4.0}$$

TABLE 9.3 DATA FROM PILOT PLANT RUNS

	A	B	C	D
			Value	Value
	Date/item	Unit	Run 1	Run 2
1	Temperature T_1	K	110.0	
2	Temperature T_2	K	115.0	
3	Temperature T_3	K	120.0	
4	Temperature T_4	K	115.0	
5	Mean temperature T_m	K	115.0	
6	Inlet carbon x_1	moles	50.0	
7	Inlet hydrogen x_2	moles	100.0	
8	Exit methane y_1	moles	20.0	
9	Exit CO_2, y_2	moles	5.0	
10	Exit CO, y_3	moles	23.0	
11	Caloric value of exit gas H	kcal/mole	1100.0	
12	Carbon closure Z	percent	4.0	

Relationships: $T_m = (T_1 + T_2 + T_3 + T_4)/4$
$H = k_1 y_1 + k_2 y_2 + k_3 y_3 + k_4 y_4$
$Z = [x_1 - (y_1 + y_2 + y_3)]/x_1$

One can therefore associate a formula with any cell. These formulas may be applied to another cell. Thus C6 and D6 have similar formulas except for a difference in the column. Facilities are provided to copy similar formulas from one cell to another.

All the calculations that need to be done have to be entered only once. This step is called the creation of a spreadsheet *template*. Thus when new columns are added or when a data item is changed, the results are immediately available.

We have only covered the basic features of a spreadsheet program. In reality spreadsheet programs come with lots more power. Some of these advanced features include

1. Graphics: the ability to create bar charts, pie charts, *x-y* plots, and so on using simple commands.
2. Database operations: the ability to sort, separate, and extract data in the table.
3. Variable column width and user-defined column formats.
4. Transfer of external data files into and out of the table (file import and file export).
5. Report writing: printing selected portions of the table in user-defined format; handling headings and tables.
6. Support of a variety of output devices such as printers, plotters, and graphics display units.

7. Ability to store very large tables. Tables that do not fit on a screen are viewed in portions. Some programs provide capability to view multiple portions through split screen operations.

Some spreadsheet packages also try to integrate other features such as word processing and the ability to communicate with other computers. This is useful if data is being collected through an RS-232C communication line, for example.

Spreadsheet Uses in DAC Systems

Spreadsheets are a very convenient way of handling repetitive calculations. Hence the important criterion is whether the calculations can be represented in the form of algebraic formulas involving cells (some spreadsheets also incorporate a certain amount of logic, so that it can be programmed). If the data collected is to be represented and analyzed the same way every time, then it would justify the purchase cost and initial time needed to set up the template.

Spreadsheet programs also offer significant advantages for displaying the data in tabular or graphical form. Thus they free the user from the drudgery of programming the computer to do the data display.

Complex calculations involving iterative loops are not suited for spreadsheet software. Such operations are better handled through specialized software designed for that purpose.

While some spreadsheet programs offer minimal database management functions, this utility is limited to relatively small volumes of data.

Realizing the popularity of the spreadsheet format for presenting data, some companies are providing software that will automatically enter data collected through DAC hardware into spreadsheet form. The LabTech Notebook offered by Laboratory Technologies is an example of such a package. Another approach you can take here is to generate date files that can be "imported" into the spreadsheet package.

9.4 WORD PROCESSING SOFTWARE

Another productivity tool that has proved itself in the office is word processing software. Word processing software aids in the creation and editing of documents.

The advantages offered by word processing lie in the ease with which changes are made in a document. Some of the advanced features include

1. the ability to make changes globally in a file
2. automatic left and right justification of text
3. automatic spelling check and correction

4. numbering and formatting of text
5. special print features such as boldface, underlining, and so on
6. the ability to "cut and paste"

Word processing software packages find applications in DAC systems for preparing custom reports, editing documents created by other programs, and editing programs (for example, FORTRAN source code).

Most word processing packages are limited to doing text processing with little or no provision for special symbols, special characters (for example, Greek letters), or graphics. Some can do special characters but will not display them on the screen (the special characters appear in coded form on the screen, but are translated at printing time). There are also technical word processors that have the ability to display them on the screen as well, albeit at the expense of some speed and efficiency.

Another consideration in the choice of word processing software is compatibility with other packages used in your office environment. Most word processors allow you to read files created in another package (this is called "importing" a file) and to create files that can be read by other packages ("exporting" of files).

9.5 INTEGRATED PACKAGES FOR DAC SYSTEMS

The need for high-quality, easy-to-use, integrated packages for scientific data analysis seems to have been recognized, and software is now appearing in the market to fill this need. The main advantages of providing an integrated (all-in-one) package are (1) the user has to learn only one consistent set of commands and (2) data can be analyzed using a succession of programs without manual transfer from one program to the next.

These software packages attempt to provide the following functions in a consistent manner.

acquire data from the hardware provided by a variety of vendors

display acquired data in graphical and tabular form

do statistical analysis of data such as finding the mean, standard deviation, and variance; apply standard correlation tests

automatically store and retrieve data in permanent medium (DBMS function)

prepare presentation graphics such as pie charts, bar graphs, x-y plots, and 3-D pictures; support a variety of hard copy and CRT devices for graphics

compute mathematical functions such as solutions of equations, matrix manipulation, matrix analysis

carry out linear and nonlinear regression (curve fitting)

carry out optimization

incorporate data reporting with formatting

use menu-driven software to minimize user-typed commands

include on-line help facilities to aid the novice

The disadvantages with this approach are that

> It requires learning a new language to operate the software.
>
> It may create and use files in formats that are incompatible with other software (unless provision is made for importing and exporting data files).
>
> It may not support one or more of the hardware components in your DAC system.
>
> It has limited flexibility in adapting the software to meet specialized requirements such as high speed or highly accurate data acquisition.

It is important to note that these packages are generally system specific with strict hardware requirements, such as

> microcomputer and operating system used
>
> graphics interfaces and graphics devices supported
>
> output printers and plotters supported
>
> minimum memory and minimum disk storage required
>
> maximum capacities in the form of speed of data acquisition, amount of data, number of channels, accuracy, and so on

A few companies providing integrated packages are cited at the end of this chapter for those interested in going this route. Packages cost in the low thousands of dollars.

CONCLUDING NOTE

The DAC field is rapidly changing with the arrival of more powerful hardware and software. A new arrival worthy of note here is the Apple Macintosh II, with its open architecture and color graphics. The recently announced Labview software from National Instruments promises to integrate DAC applications with the rest of the computer system, thus making the transition of the data from the sensor to the final report smooth and easy. This is an example where both the software and hardware can be treated as a completely integrated unit.

SUMMARY

The objective of this chapter was to explore some of the alternative software that is available today to facilitate data management and analysis. Database management systems are suited for repetitive handling of large amounts of similar data. Spreadsheet packages are a convenient way to do repetitive calculations, display data in tabular format, and generate graphs or reports. Finally, integrated software packages attempt to provide an all-in-one system so that the user does not have to master different packages or shuffle data between programs. In addition to these, there are hundreds of software packages for specific applications. A few companies that market such software are listed at the end of this chapter.

REVIEW QUESTIONS

1. What is the difference between DBMS and LIMS?
2. List some requirements of data analysis in a DAC system.
3. Cite some laboratory applications where a spreadsheet program can be used.
4. Develop a spreadsheet table like the one shown in Table 9.3 for representing a home budget.
5. Analyze the current data handling requirements in your laboratory or organization and evaluate the use of DBMS, spreadsheet, and integrated software packages.

REFERENCES

The book by Dologite is an excellent introduction to DBMS, spreadsheet packages, and other business application packages.

DOLOGITE, D. G. *Using Small Business Computers*. Englewood Cliffs, NJ: Prentice-Hall, 1984.

The following book surveys and rates various DBMS programs available for the IBM PC:

EMERSON, S. L., AND M. DARNOVSKY. *Database for the IBM PC*. Reading, MA: Addison-Wesley, 1984.

The following articles describe various aspects of LIMS (laboratory information systems):

DESSY, R. E. "Laboratory Information Management Systems." *Analytical Chemistry* 55, no. 1 (1983): 70A–80A.

GOLDEN, J. H. "Economics of Laboratory Information Systems." *Instruments and Computers,* May 1985, 13–17.

SLABIN, S. S., M. J. MILANO, AND G. W. LIESEGANG. "Future Trends in Laboratory Computing." *Instruments and Computers,* June 1985, 30–37.

The following issue of *Science Software Quarterly* (published by the Center for Environmental Studies, Arizona State University, Tempe) has two articles describing integrated software packages for the laboratory:

Science Software Quarterly 2, no. 2 (1985).

LIST OF SOFTWARE VENDORS

The following is a partial listing of companies that market software for data acquisition and control using microcomputers. In addition, the many manufacturers of interfacing hardware also market compatible software. Complete addresses can be found in Appendix B.

BBN Software Products Corp.

Centaurus Software, Inc.

CET Research Group, Ltd.

Dynamic Solutions Corp.

Gantt Systems, Inc.

Heuristics, Inc.

Hewlett-Packard

Interactive Microwave, Inc.

Laboratory Technologies, Inc.

Macmillan Software Co.

Radian Corp.

The Scientific Press

Small Business Computers of New England

Unkel Software, Inc.

10

Communications
and Networking

10.1 DATA COMMUNICATION NEEDS IN DAC SYSTEMS

As instruments and DAC systems become computerized, the need for instruments and computers to transfer digital information among them will become more and more important. The common communication requirements today involve the following:

1. communicating data acquired by the DAC system to a mainframe computer
2. accessing and transferring data stored in a mainframe to the DAC computer
3. communicating with an instrument that already has a microprocessor installed in it
4. sharing an expensive peripheral device such as a laserprinter with a number of other computers

As we will see, there are a variety of ways in which this communication link can be accomplished. The variations arise due to different requirements among the systems as well as due to different communication standards followed by each computer manufacturer. Since DAC users typically purchase equipment from more than one vendor, establishing the proper communication link is often a tricky problem. There have been numerous attempts to arrive at some industrywide standard that will simplify this problem, and the momentum toward establishing one is increasing.

It may be noted here that this problem of providing communication links between computers is not limited to DAC systems, but is rather part of the more general problem of linking together all types of digital devices (for example, printers, terminals, plotters, tape drives, disk drives, and so on).

We begin by listing a few examples that illustrate the need for communication in

DAC systems. This is followed by a discussion of the technology used in communication and the two communication standards that are in wide use today.

Example 1

A DAC system is designed to acquire data from a coal gasification pilot plant. Detailed temperature profiles of the reactor and exit gas compositions are acquired by the DAC system and stored on a floppy disk. This data must be plotted and compared with the model predictions. The model is too large to fit into the microcomputer and resides on a minicomputer located in the same building.

The problem can be solved by establishing a link between the two computers by means of a twisted-pair wire. A communications card is needed for the microcomputer. The card and the software that came with it allow the microcomputer to behave like a terminal to the minicomputer, thus allowing transfer of data files back and forth.

The user runs the communications software to establish the terminal emulation mode in the microcomputer. He or she then logs on to the minicomputer and is able to transfer files from the microcomputer, using the capabilities of the communications software.

Example 2

The user of a DAC system needs to obtain information from a databank stored in the corporate mainframe computer located 100 miles away. Similarly, daily log summaries must be sent to the mainframe.

This can be solved by first acquiring a device called a *modem* on the microcomputer. This is plugged into the motherboard of the computer on one of the expansion slots provided. The modem links with the telephone jack. Software provided by the modem manufacturer can be used to emulate a variety of terminals.

The communication link is established with the mainframe computer through one of the dial-up lines provided at the mainframe. The user simply types in the number and the modem automatically dials, waits for an appropriate response, and then enters the terminal emulation mode. The keys of the microcomputer now take on different meanings based on the terminal type chosen.

The user logs on to the mainframe computer, obtains information from the mainframe databank, and then transfers the log summary files, prepared earlier, to the mainframe. Since the communications software is all menu-driven, the user does not have to learn any new commands to use the system.

Example 3

A laboratory has two mass spectroscopy instruments. Each one was acquired with an option called an IEEE-488 interface, which the manufacturer intended for communicating the results of the instrument to another device. The manufacturer also provided the commands necessary to transfer data from the instrument.

The requirement now is to consolidate the results from the two mass specs in a microcomputer where further data analysis could be carried out.

To accomplish this the user acquired a card for the microcomputer called the IEEE-488 interface card. The manufacturer of this card provided the software necessary to set up the protocol to activate an IEEE-488 bus. The mass specs could then be linked with the microcomputer using a cable also made specifically for IEEE-488 interfaces.

Using the manuals provided by the mass spec manufacturer and the IEEE-488 interface card manufacturer, the user was able to write programs in BASIC that effected the data transfer. The IEEE bus also provides the capacity to link with other instruments if necessary at a future date.

Example 4

Company XYZ Inc. has a number of DAC systems. The data acquired by these DAC systems needs to be shared among the various users. Thus user A needs to know the results of a test conducted by user B, and so on. Also, the company recently acquired an expensive letter quality printer for sending out summary reports to customers. It is desirable to make this device accessible to all the users as well.

The problem was solved by consulting with a company that manufactured hardware and software for setting up what are called local area networks (LANs). This meant laying a coaxial cable linking all the DAC system microcomputers and the printer. One of the micros served as the network controller. Interface boards had to be acquired for all the micros to link to the cable. The networking software was menu-driven and allowed transfer of data files back and forth. An additional feature that came with the LAN was the ability for the users to send messages to each other.

10.2 COMMUNICATION

Suppose person A wants to talk to person B in a physically different location. Before they can establish a communication link, they must agree on the following:

1. the physical medium of communication (telephone, CB radio, television, writing, and so forth)
2. the language used
3. a communication protocol (who talks first, how to interpret it, and so on)

The problems in establishing a communication link between two devices are similar. Before a link can be established, the two devices must agree on

1. the physical (electrical) connection method linking the two devices
2. the communication code (the meaning of each byte of information transmitted)
3. the communications protocol (the method by which the talker and listener establish the link and transfer bytes of data back and forth)

Physical Linking Methods

Physical linking methods can be categorized into two major types, *parallel* and *serial*. In parallel communication data is transmitted one byte at a time, all 8 bits simultaneously along 8 different wires. In addition, some additional lines are usually required for timing and control purposes. The use of these timing and control lines differs between manufac-turers. One standard proposed for parallel communication is the IEEE-488 standard. It appears to be emerging as a standard for parallel communications in the laboratory. This standard uses special interconnecting cables to link various devices. Another widely used standard for parallel connection is the Centronics Parallel Interface, which is used to physically connect printers and proximate computers. Figure 10.1 illustrates the use of a parallel communication link between two devices.

In serial communication data is transmitted 1 bit at a time. Thus 1 byte is broken up into 8 bits, and these bits are sent over a single line at a predetermined rate. Bytes are separated from each other using start bits and stop bits. As with parallel transmissions, a few extra lines are required for control purposes. Timing is usually controlled by fixing the rate of transmission at both ends of the communication link. As with parallel commu-nication, there is one standard that is widely followed in serial communication (this is the RS-232C standard).

Figure 10.2 illustrates the serial link between two devices. The serial interface boards capture data from the bus appearing in parallel form and then transmit one bit at a time. The procedure is reversed when receiving information.

Successive bytes are separated by start and stop bits, as shown in Figure 10.3. The two devices must agree on such items as number of stop bits, transmission rate, voltage levels used, error checking procedures, control lines used, and so on. This is where the standard comes in.

Serial links can also be established over longer distances using telephone links. In this case a modem is used to link the serial line to the telephone line. This is illustrated in Figure 10.4. The RS-232C standard was originally developed to define the link between the computer and the modem

Because of the cost of wiring, serial links are cheaper to establish. Thus almost all communications over distances longer than a few meters are done using some type of serial link. Serial links are used to establish communication between computer, printer, plotter, intelligent instruments, and so on.

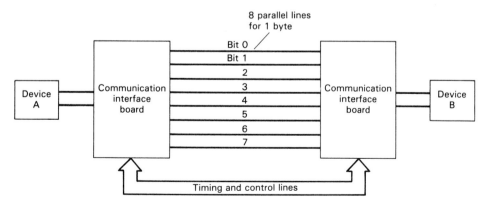

Figure 10.1   Parallel communication

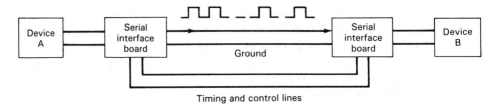

Figure 10.2 Serial data communication

The modem converts binary signals from the serial interface to modulated frequency signals that are transmitted over the phone lines. Typically

For transmitting modem: "0" = 1070 Hz (low band)
                             "1" = 1270 Hz
For receiving modem: "0" = 2025 Hz (high band)
                           "1" = 2225 Hz

There are three kinds of modems on the market today.

External modems are of the type shown in Figure 10.4. These modems link to the telephone jack on one side and a serial interface on the other side.

Internal modems combine the function of the serial interface and the modem into a single card that plugs into the expansion slots on the motherboard of the microcomputer. These offer cost advantages, but one of the expansion slots must be dedicated for telephone communication.

The third class of modems use what are known as *acoustic couplers,* which are then coupled with the telephone mouthpiece. The binary signals are first converted to voice frequencies that are transmitted by the telephone. These devices are more susceptible to disturbances than direct-wired modems and hence are not recommended for high-speed transmission of data.

The speed of transmission in serial mode is measured in terms of bits/sec or the *baud rate.* Typical baud rates in use are 110, 300, 1200, 4800, 9600, and 19,200. Since

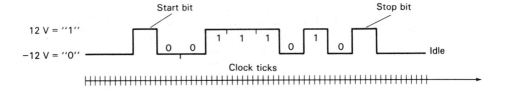

Byte transmitter: "00111010"

Figure 10.3 Serial transmission of one byte

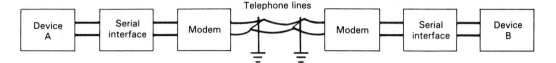

Figure 10.4   Data communication via telephone lines

each byte takes 10 or 11 bits (8 data, 1 start, and 1 or 2 stop bits), the speed of transmission in terms of characters/sec is roughly a tenth of the baud rate.

Normal voice grade telephone lines are generally satisfactory for speeds up to 1200 baud. To get an idea of what this speed means, a page on the IBM PC contains 25 lines × 80 characters/line = 2000 characters. Thus at 1200 baud approximately 17 sec is required to fill a screen. This is reasonably fast for moderate applications, but some people find it too slow when working with full-screen editors.

Dedicated phone lines can be leased from the telephone company that allow transmission up to 19,200 baud. Also, if the serial link is established directly without going through the phone line, then higher baud rates are feasible.

Another choice that is usually available with telephone communication is whether to use simplex, half duplex, or full duplex. This must be set to be the same at both ends of the communication link. In simplex mode, communication can take place only in one direction, fixed a priori. In half duplex mode, communication is possible in both directions, but in only one direction at a time. In full duplex (the usual choice), communication is possible in both directions at the same time. Most modems today allow this option to be selected by the user.

Communications Code

In order for the two devices communicating with each other to understand each other, they must agree on how the bits and bytes are to be interpreted. The interpretation of each byte into alphanumeric information is called the *communications code*.

Currently there are two widely used ways of coding alphanumeric information into bytes. These are *ASCII (American Standard Code for Information Interchange)* and *EBCDIC (Extended Binary Coded Decimal Interchange Code)*. ASCII Code, also known as *ANSI Code,* is followed in microcomputers. EBCDIC is used mainly by IBM mainframe computers.

ASCII uses only 7 bits and defines 127 characters (A–Z uppercase and lowercase, 0–9, and a number of special characters). The eighth bit may be used to define additional graphics characters, as is done in the IBM PC, or may be used to check for errors during transmission. In the latter case, this bit is called a *parity bit*. It is used to make the total number of 1s in a transmitted byte even (even parity) or odd (odd parity). Thus the receiver can check to see if the byte was received intact. The complete ASCII and EBCDIC codes are given in many books (such as the one by Mellichamp listed in the reference sections of earlier chapters).

A third, but now obsolete, way of coding numeric data is the *BCD* (*binary coded decimal*). Here decimal numbers are converted to binary using 4 bits to represent each decimal digit form. For example, the decimal number 589 will be represented in BCD as

$$0101 \ 1000 \ 1001$$

Note that 0101 in binary is 5, 1000 is 8, and 1001 is 9. Many laboratory instruments used to output data in BCD format.

Communications Protocol

Before communications can begin and during the communication period, the two devices must agree on how the data will be transmitted. This is accomplished through the control lines and/or through special transmitted characters. This process is called the *communications protocol*.

At low baud rates (<19,200) an *asynchronous transmission* protocol is used. The control lines are used to indicate whether each device is ready for data communication. The data are sent one byte at a time with the start and stop bits added. These extra bits make transmission inefficient.

If higher baud rates are desired, we could purchase interfaces that are capable of communication using a *synchronous protocol*. Here special characters are transmitted at the beginning to synchronize the two devices. Bytes are sent in packets of 250 or more with no start and stop bits in between. At the end of a packet, special error checking bytes and termination characters are sent. Two commonly used synchronous protocols are (1) *BISYNC* (*binary synchronous communication protocol*), developed and used by IBM to link high-speed terminals, and (2) *HDLC* (*high level data link control*), developed by the International Standards Organization.

Note that the interface hardware and software required in the synchronous transmission mode are quite different and generally cost more. Data rates up to 500,000 bits/sec are achievable using synchronous transmission hardware.

10.3 THE RS-232C SERIAL COMMUNICATION STANDARD

The RS-232C (Recommended Standard-232C, Electronic Industries Association) was originally proposed for standardizing the pin connections and voltage levels used for connecting a computer (called the *DTE* or *data terminal equipment*) to a communications device (called *DCE* or *data communications equipment*). Subsets of the standard are now widely used by computer peripheral and instrument manufacturers to establish communication links. Since the full standard is often not required or used, there may be slight differences in the way it is implemented in each device. This is a source of confusion, since two devices, both of which claim to follow the standard, cannot simply be connected to each other without checking whether both follow the same subset of the standard.

The RS-232 standard defines a 25-pin connection at each end. This is usually called the *RS-232 interface connector* and is illustrated in Figure 10.5. Not all 25 pins are used.

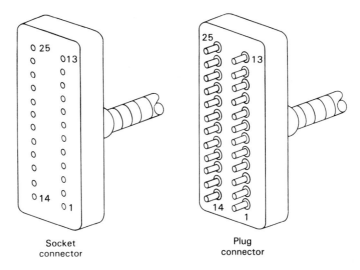

Figure 10.5   RS-232C interface connectors

In fact some implementations may use as few as 3 of these wires to complete the connection. The trick is to know which ones are needed.

The commonly used pins and their uses are given below:

Pin 1:   This is a protective ground that is also used as a shield.

Pin 2:   Transmitted data. This is the line used by the DTE to send out signals. This is connected to pin 2 of the DCE, which receives data on this line.

Pin 3:   Received data. This line carries incoming signals to the DTE.

Pins 4 and 5:   Request to send and clear to send. Used in half duplex operation only. If this line is high (on), it indicates that the device is ready to receive data. Pin 4 is used by DTE and 5 by DCE. In full duplex these lines are always held high.

Pin 6:   Data set ready. Signal used by DCE to indicate that it is ready.

Pin 7:   Signal ground.

Pin 8:   Carrier detect. Signal generated by DCE to indicate the validity of the line connection.

Pin 20:   Data terminal ready. The counterpart of pin 6. Signal generated by DTE.

The distinction between DTE and DCE is a confusing one. An RS-232 device interface may be configured as either one. The device manual should indicate which way it is. Most computers use DTE. Modems use DCE. Printers use DCE or DTE. DTE receive incoming signals on pin 3 and send out data on pin 2. The reverse is true for DCE.

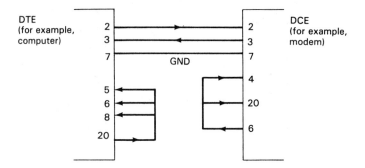

Figure 10.6 A null modem connection

    DTE is usually configured with a 25-pin plug, whereas DCE is usually configured with a 25-pin socket.

    In almost 99% of the cases only pins 2, 3, and 7 are required. The control lines are not used. In this case a cheater connection of the type known as a *null modem* may be used (see Figure 10.6). In this case lines 5, 6, and 8 of the DTE are kept active by linking to line 20. Similarly, lines 4 and 20 of the DCE are kept active by linking to line 6.

    Occasionally it is desirable to connect a computer to another computer (that is, DTE to another DTE). This may be done using a cross-wired cable, as shown in Figure 10.7.

    The discussion above is limited to asynchronous communication between two devices. During synchronous communication many other control lines are used. For a detailed discussion of these and other subjects related to RS-232, see Seyer (1984). This reference also provides the connections for a wide variety of microcomputers and peripheral devices.

    A device known as an "RS-232C Breakout Box" is available from electronics supply shops for monitoring the signals from an RS-232C interface. It may be used as a diagnostic tool for monitoring the status of various lines.

    The voltages used in this standard (for indicating high/low levels) are higher than the usual TTL voltages used within the computer. The standard dictates the following:

Logic state	Voltage	Name
0	−3 to −25 V	Mark
1	+3 to +25 V	Space

These levels allow greater noise immunity. The standard specifies a maximum distance of 30 m between equipment and a maximum data transfer rate of 20,000 bits/sec.

    Two other standards, RS-422A and RS-423, have been approved by the EIA for connection over longer distances. These are not as widely used as the RS-232C standard. Possible applications include process control where the DAC systems may be located several thousand feet apart.

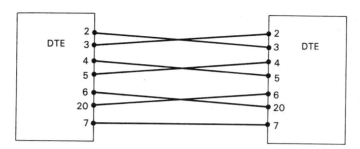

Figure 10.7   A cross-wired cable for connecting a DTE to another DTE

10.4 THE IEEE-488 STANDARD

The disadvantages with RS-232 serial communication are that data transfer rates are slow and one interface is required at the microcomputer for each serial communication device. Microcomputers such as the IBM PC are limited to two serial interfaces by the operating system. This means your PC can talk to only two serial devices at any time. Since many printers and plotters also use serial interface, one soon uses up the two available ports.

One solution around this is to use the IEEE-488 parallel interface. This interface was originally proposed by Hewlett-Packard, and is also known as

Hewlett-Packard interface bus (HPIB)

General-purpose interface bus (GPIB)

ANSI bus

IEC-625-1 bus (in Europe)

This bus was adopted by the IEEE (Institute of Electrical and Electronics Engineers) in 1978.

The use of the IEEE-488 bus is illustrated in Figure 10.8. The bus requires an

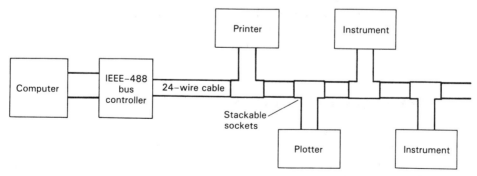

Figure 10.8   Structure of IEEE-488 network

interface on the computer called the *IEEE-488 interface controller*. Each device on the bus must also have an IEEE-488 interface built in. In addition, specific software is required to set up the protocol and start the communication between devices.

The standard defines a 24-wire cable (this cable is rather expensive), out of which 8 bits are used for data, 8 for control, and the remainder for shielding and grounding. A maximum cable length of 20 m is supported (maximum of 2 m between devices), and up to 15 devices may be linked with the network. Of these at least half must be powered on for the bus to work. Data rates of up to 1 Mb/sec may be used. TTL levels are used. The standard specifies the mechanical and electrical characteristics of the interface connectors and the functions of the controller.

The devices on the bus could be of the following types:

Controller:	Controls the activities of the bus. Is able to talk, listen, and control. Only one controller is allowed. Example: a microcomputer.
Talker:	Only sends information of the bus, for example, a frequency counter. Only one device may talk at any time. Examples: digital thermometer, digital voltmeter.
Listener:	Only receives data from the data bus. Up to 15 active listeners are permitted on the line. Examples: printers, plotters.
Talker/listener:	Able to send and receive information. Examples: microcomputers, disk drives, intelligent instruments.

Data on the bus is ASCII coded and hence uses only 7 bits. The data bus is also used to send device addresses and commands to devices. The standard specifies the type of commands used.

Communication can normally be achieved through high-level languages such as BASIC. When a device wants to communicate, it asserts one of the control lines. The controller then polls each device to see who wants to talk. After the device to talk has been identified, the controller determines who the listener is and puts that device into listen mode. The controller then releases the data bus to effect the transfer. After the data transfer is complete, the controller takes charge of the bus again.

Software for controlling the data transfer is usually provided by the manufacturers who make the controller boards. Generally this software is in the form of subroutines that can be activated from a high-level language such as BASIC or FORTRAN.

Advantages and Disadvantages of the IEEE-488 Bus

This type of communication link is suited for tying together devices and instruments in close proximity. It costs about $1000 or so to obtain this interface as an option on an instrument. And it may not be available on all instruments. The microcomputer used should have the bus controller, and again, not all microcomputers may have this available.

IEEE-488 bus controllers are available for most popular microcomputers. The Commodore Pet microcomputer comes with this option built in.

The big advantages are the high speed of data transfer and the ability to string up to 15 devices. This is a good way of sharing expensive peripherals. This interface bus was primarily developed for laboratory instrumentation, and this is where it will find the most applications.

10.5 NETWORKING

So far we have considered mainly the linking of intelligent devices to one computer. Now we begin to address the issue of linking many computers. This is commonly referred to as *networking*.

There are two types of networking. *Local area networks* or *LANs* are concerned with the networking of computers that are physically proximate, such as microcomputers within a laboratory or an office. *Wide area networks* or *WANs* are concerned with linking computers that are geographically distributed.

Some techniques of wide area networking were already discussed above. The dialing up of a remote host mainframe from a micro using a modem is an example of a wide area network.

Figure 10.9 shows three common architectures used in developing networks. In a *star* network, the microcomputers are linked to a central host computer, which acts as an intermediary in the transactions. This type of network structure is susceptible to failure because of the centralized transaction feature. Since the data traffic on any one line is limited, the connection may be achieved using inexpensive twisted-pair wiring. Data rates up to 50,000 bits/sec are supported on such lines.

In a *bus* network, a single coaxial cable is used to handle all the transactions. Data rates up to 10 Mb/sec are feasible with a coaxial cable. However, a problem here is the conflict that arises due to contention for a common resource by multiple users. One form of technology that has been developed to handle this problem is called *CSMA/CD* (*carrier sense, multiple access/collision detect*), which is employed in the Ethernet Scheme marketed by Xerox Corporation. Each device in the network has a unique address and uses the network as long as there is no conflict. In case of conflict, each device waits for a random period before attempting to use the bus again. Each device on the bus listens to the data transactions on the bus and captures only those addressed to itself.

A *ring* network uses a token that goes around continuously. The token is a special code of binary bits. A device can use the network only when it has possession of the token. Some speed is sacrificed as a result.

The costs associated with setting up a network consist of those for

cabling
network interface hardware required for each device on the network
network software

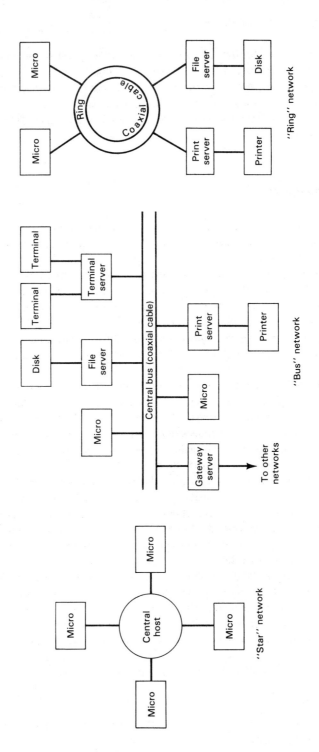

Figure 10.9 The three types of networks

"Ring" network

Ring

Coaxial cable

Micro

Micro

File server

Disk

Print server

Printer

Terminal

Terminal

Terminal server

Disk

File server

Micro

Central bus (coaxial cable)

Gateway server

To other networks

Micro

Print server

Printer

"Bus" network

Micro

Micro

Central host

Micro

Micro

"Star" network

The uses of a network are to

> send messages to other users
> share peripherals
> share data files and databases
> avoid duplication of data and software

Baseband Versus Broadband

The use of a single channel on the coaxial cable to set up a network is referred to as *baseband* technology. The limiting factor with a single channel is the maximum data transfer rate. To overcome this difficulty, a technology that involves frequency division multiplexing is used to divide a single cable into multiple channels, each channel communicating at a certain frequency. Using this broadband technology, up to 32 channels of communication may be set up on a single coaxial cable. This is probably going to be the future trend with networking. Broadband transmission requires higher-quality coaxial cables such as those used in cable TV.

CONCLUDING REMARKS

In practice, a hierarchy of networks may be needed in an organization. Locally, within an office or laboratory, a baseband network may be used to link the microcomputers. Through the use of network gateway interfaces, this network may be linked to a larger companywide broadband network connecting minis and mainframes.

LANs and WANs are still in a state of development, with competing but conflicting technologies offered by different manufacturers. The International Standards Organization is developing some standards to cover the networking of computers. In factory automation, the manufacturing automation protocol (MAP) developed by General Motors is now gaining wide acceptance.

SUMMARY

The need for data communication arises frequently in DAC systems because of the need to

> share information
> share software
> share expensive peripherals
> transfer data from one computer to another

Communication between devices can be set up in a number of ways. The simplest uses an RS-232 serial interface to link the two devices. This is limited to communication between two devices. The IEEE-488 bus may be employed for linking up to 15 physically proximate devices if each device can be fitted with an interface to this bus. Transfer rates up to 1 megabit/sec may be achieved using this network.

Finally, we talked about networking computers locally and over a wide area. Several companies have the hardware and software to accomplish networking, but these are generally not compatible with each other. It is possible to develop gateway links between networks. Ultimately, every company will have many small and large networks with interconnections.

REVIEW QUESTIONS

1. A DAC user wants to transfer the data acquired on the microcomputer to a mainframe. Suggest alternative ways in which this may be accomplished if
   (a) Data items to be transferred are only a few hundred in number and the transfer is done infrequently.
   (b) Large volumes of data must be transferred at frequent intervals.
2. A department has a minicomputer and several microcomputers. Each microcomputer is dedicated to do a DAC function. Suggest ways in which the minicomputer and microcomputers may be linked so that data can be transferred between microcomputers and between the minicomputer and the microcomputers.
3. A company is about to acquire several intelligent instruments. The instrument manufacturer is offering the option of either an RS-232C interface or an IEEE-488 bus interface on the instrument. Which should be picked and why? What other information will you need to make a decision?
4. Contact several companies offering networking for the IBM PC. Compare and contrast their features, such as speed, cost of cabling, cost of software, cost of interface cards, maximum data transfer rates, and so on.
5. What hardware and software will you need to purchase to establish a link between your microcomputer and a computer located several hundred miles away? What are the maximum data transfer rates achievable with the commercially available hardware?
6. What is the difference between baseband and broadband networks?

REFERENCES

For readers interested in understanding the RS-232C interface connection in greater detail, the book by Seyer is recommended.

SEYER, M.D. *RS-232 Made Easy*. Englewood Cliffs, NJ: Prentice-Hall, 1984.
   This book explains, in simple terms, the protocols used for both synchronous and asynchronous interfaces using this standard.

STONE, H. S. *Microcomputer Interfacing.* Reading, MA: Addison-Wesley, 1982.
  This book gets into some of the hardware aspects of building both parallel and serial interfaces, including the RS-232C and the IEEE-488 standard.

ELECTRONIC INDUSTRIES ASSOCIATION. *Interface Between Data Terminal Equipment and Data Communication Equipment Employing Serial Binary Data Interchange.* EIA Standard RS-232C, 1969. (Available from Electronic Industries Association, 2001 I Street, NW, Washington, DC 20006.)

INSTITUTE OF ELECTRICAL AND ELECTRONICS ENGINEERS. *IEEE Standard for Digital Interface for Programmable Instrumentation.* IEEE Standard 488-1975, IEEE Standard 488-1978. (Available from Institute of Electrical and Electronics Engineers, 345 E. 47th St., New York, NY 10017.)
  The two references above give the official wording of the two standards discussed in this chapter.

DESSEY, R. E. "Local Area Networks: Part I." *Analytical Chemistry* (54), no. 11, (September 1982): 1167A–1182A.
  This article and its sequel explain the applications of networking in a laboratory environment.

LIST OF MANUFACTURERS

The following is a partial list of companies that market communication products for DAC application needs. Complete addresses can be found in Appendix B.

  Analog Devices
  Burr-Brown Corp.
  Capital Equipment Corp.
  Connecticut Microcomputer
  Cyber Research, Inc.
  Hewlett-Packard
  IO Tech
  Motorola Semiconductor Products, Inc.
  National Instruments
  Real-Time Devices, Inc.

11

Design, Selection, and Implementation of DAC Systems

11.1 INTRODUCTION

In this chapter we would like to address the project management procedures for implementing a DAC system. Approaching the project in a systematic manner is important to ensure the successful completion and operation of the DAC system. The various steps involved in a DAC system development project are outlined in this chapter, with some useful tips and possible pitfalls.

Figure 11.1 summarizes the numerous steps involved in the execution of a DAC system project. The project starts with the specifications of the user's requirements. A set of *functional specifications* of the DAC system is drawn up in consultation with the user. These functional specifications form the basis for the design of DAC systems. The designs are outlined in the form of a document called *system specifications*.

The system specifications are used to survey the market for the availability of suitable hardware and software. Sometimes this may suggest some minor modifications to the design to accommodate available hardware and software and to reduce costs.

The next step in the project execution is the selection of system components and vendors who can supply these components. Plans must be made to develop those components that are not available in the market. These various components are put together and tested for system integrity and performance. Maintenance procedures must be developed. The final system must be documented from the point of view of the user, the system maintenance people, and the project management team.

In the following sections, each of the project management activities cited above is explained in detail.

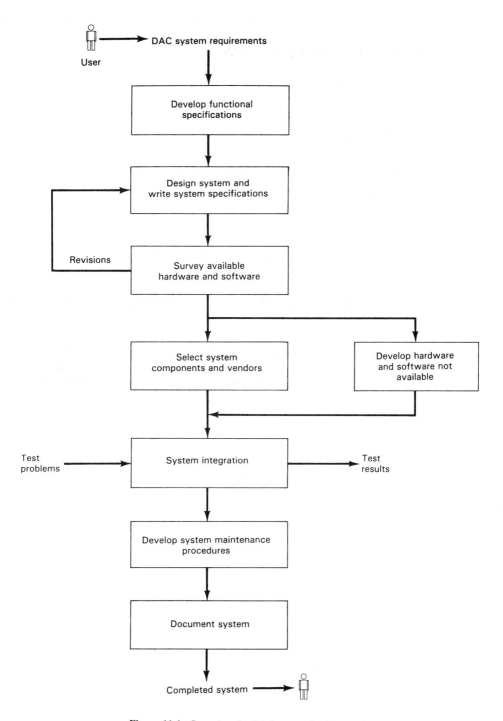

Figure 11.1 Procedure for DAC system implementation

11.2 FUNCTIONAL SPECIFICATIONS

The system design begins with a meeting between the design team and the users of the proposed DAC system. The questions to be raised initially are

What are the *objectives* of the DAC system?

What are the *basic requirements*?

What are other desirable features?

What are the measurements to be taken and what control features are needed in the DAC system?

What further processing of the data is required?

The result of this session is a document called the functional specifications of the DAC system. The various components of this document are described next.

1. Statement of objectives.   This is a brief paragraph summarizing the objectives of the proposed DAC system.

2. Input/output description.   This should list all the different input and output signals to be processed by the DAC system. It should identify the origin and nature of each input (analog, digital, pulse, other), expected frequency content (that is, range of frequencies present in the signal), noise level, range (the maximum and minimum values of signal), and required frequency of sampling. The kinds of outputs to be sent out from the DAC system, the type of actuators to be used, and the frequency of updating needed should also be identified.

3. Data analysis requirements.   This should list the data analysis functions expected of the DAC system, such as

noise filtering

data regression

statistical analysis

model fitting

Data analysis may be performed in three ways:

1. on-line (during data acquisition)
2. off-line at the microcomputer
3. off-line at a different computer

The on-line analysis should be carefully weighed against the time available between measurements and control functions. If the analysis is not urgent, defer it until the data acquisition and control functions can be turned off. Similarly, the decision between doing the analysis on the microcomputer versus another computer should be made after evaluating the costs and time requirements of both options.

4. Data communication requirements

Does data have to be transmitted elsewhere? If so, how much data? What is the destination?

What are the means of communication at the receiving end?

Are there intelligent instruments that have to be interfaced to the computer, and if so, what kind of communication interfaces do these instruments have?

Is communication via the telephone lines needed? If so, at what data rate?

5. Data storage and retrieval requirements

How much data is generated per run? per day?

How much data is to be saved per run? per day? for how long?

How often does data have to be retrieved (for display, analysis, report generation, and so on)?

Will other users require access to the data? simultaneously?

Should data be protected? What are acceptable means of protection?

6. Data display and report writing functions

How would users display the data?

Does it require color?

Will graphical displays be desirable? If so, are hard copies necessary?

What kind of reports are needed? How often? What is their data content?

Are letter quality reports desirable?

Will users be doing considerable report writing? If so, is word processing capability needed?

7. Operator communication requirements

What will be the background of operators who will use the system?

How is the operator expected to interact with the DAC system before, during, and after a run?

What kind of information should be provided to the operator?

What kind of information is expected to be entered by the operator?

Are alarms necessary? What type and how many?

11.3 SYSTEM SPECIFICATIONS

The functional specifications developed above form the basis for the design of the DAC system. The system requirements will guide in the selection of appropriate hardware and software tools. The result is another document, called system specifications. The various components of this document are described next.

1. Computer system specifications.   This should specify the following items:

CPU word length (8-bit, 16-bit, or 32-bit)

memory (number of kilobytes required)

permanent storage (during a run, archival)

input devices (keyboard, mouse, touchscreen, and so on)

output devices (printer, plotter, CRT, and so forth)

communication interfaces (modem, IEEE-488, RS-232C, and so on)

2. Computer/process interface specifications.   This consists of a description of each quantity to be measured and each signal to be interfaced to the computer. For input items the following items are desirable:

sensor type

signal conditioning needed

sampling frequency

range of signal

data type (digital, analog, pulse, BCD, and so on)

accuracy desired

For output signals the following items are desirable:

data type (digital, analog, current, voltage, pulse, BCD, and so on)

time interval between output updates

actuator type used (solenoid, relay, pneumatic)

range of output

accuracy desired

3. Software specifications.   This should list the requirements expected of the software in terms of

> operating system (single or multitasking, compatibility with existing programs, file compatibility, availability of software)
>
> data analysis (sensor calibration, conversion to engineering units, noise filtering, peak detection and integration, curve fitting, data regression, statistical tests)
>
> data management (how much data, how many simultaneous users, types of data, security features, retrieval requirements)
>
> word processing (report writing) requirements
>
> programming languages desired
>
> compatibility with some existing hardware or other software

11.4 SYSTEM SELECTION

Selecting the hardware and software that meet the system specifications is an iterative process involving a number of considerations. The iterations involve revising the original system specifications on the basis of cost, availability, and ease of implementation.

Market Survey

The selection process begins with a survey of what is available on the market. The system specifications are used as a basis for surveying the market to determine the availability and cost of hardware and software that meet the specifications.

There are a variety of sources that carry information on microcomputers. A good place to start is with trade magazines that carry advertisements on products in this area. Appendix A lists a variety of publications that focus their attention on the microcomputer application area. Of these, two publications, *Personal Engineering and Instrumentation News* and *Intelligent Instruments and Computers,* concentrate heavily on data acquisition and control applications of microcomputers.

Appendix B contains a partial list of manufacturers who have products in the DAC field. Many of them have catalog publications in the area.

Another good source of information on products are the trade fairs organized by various professional societies, such as the Instrument Society of America, the Institute of Electrical and Electronics Engineers, the American Chemical Society, the American Institute of Chemical Engineers, the American Society of Mechanical Engineers, and so on. These trade fairs and equipment shows are announced in trade journals.

User groups are good sources for obtaining firsthand information from other people. User groups for popular computers are now available in most major cities. In large companies, such user groups may be formed in-house. This then becomes a point to establish contacts with people who have applications similar to your own.

Guidelines for Selection

It is preferable to buy hardware and software in the marketplace rather than develop it in-house. The reasons are that (1) most users tend to underestimate the time and effort required to build, test, and install hardware and software; (2) the maintenance of items built in-house is difficult due to personnel changeover; (3) the economics of large-scale production are not available when building systems in-house; (4) software purchase prices are generally only a fraction of the development cost; (5) most in-house systems are built for a specific project or application and hence are less adaptable when the project requirements change or when the project is over.

There may be instances when building the hardware or software in-house is a necessity, however. This is particularly true if the application is very specialized in nature, such as very high-speed data acquisition (> 50 KHz) or very accurate data acquisitions. Building short programs for specific needs is an acceptable approach in this case.

In selecting a microcomputer system, it is advisable to consider the popular families of microcomputers first. You are more likely to find a wide selection of hardware and software for these systems. The selection of the microcomputer system will automatically narrow down the choice of available hardware and software. Other important criteria for selection are

cost

maintenance support

capability for future expansion

availability of spare parts

physical proximity of service centers

hardware used in other parts of your company or organization

reputation of the manufacturer (how long has it been in business?)

The maintenance and customer support provided by the manufacturer is an important consideration in the selection of hardware and software. If other computer systems are used in-house, then users might prove to be a good source of technical support and spare parts. In an emergency you might be able to swap boards, software, and other programs.

The application of the above criteria should narrow down the field of possible candidates to a few. More detailed evaluation, including demonstrations and benchmark tests, can then be conducted to make a final choice.

If it turns out that none of the available systems meets the specified requirements, one might consider reviewing and altering the design specifications in consultation with the user. There is usually some room for negotiation here. The other alternative is to build the hardware and software in-house.

Building hardware in-house will require someone familiar with analog and digital electronics. Areas of expertise needed are in microcomputer hardware interfacing, analog signal conditioning, and assembly language programming. Careful attention should be paid to extensively document systems built in-house, since the original designer may not be available for maintenance and repair. The system should be thoroughly tested, and if it is a critical item, a duplicate should also be made to provide backup in case of component failure. The major cost of building systems in-house is in labor.

Software prepared in-house should similarly be tested and be well documented both internally (within the software) and externally. The other important considerations are to

1. Use a high-level language whenever possible. Candidates are BASIC (readily available, suited for small programs), FORTRAN (popular for scientific computing), and C.
2. Use a standard form of the language if such standards exist. This will make it easier to transfer programs to another computer system at a future date.
3. Make the system user-friendly. Anticipate operator mistakes and provide corrective actions. Always check input data for consistency, and build in error recovery schemes.
4. Try to maintain modularity in the software by breaking up the program into small self-contained modules. No module should be larger than a few hundred lines of code.
5. Use structured programming methodology.
6. Require extensive documentation in the form of user manuals, system manuals, and internal documentation.

11.5 IMPLEMENTATION AND TESTING

Installation should proceed in steps. First each module should be tested individually as it is purchased or developed. Most manufacturers provide diagnostic and test programs to check the operation of the hardware and software.

After each component has been tested, begin system integration by assembling the components one at a time. One frequent source of problems at this stage is incompatibility of components or systems, particularly if they are made by different manufacturers. If possible, develop a series of routine tests that can be conducted to isolate problem components. This will come in handy for future maintenance of the system. Another source of problems here is improper grounding and shielding of cables. Noise-generated problems will be sporadic in nature and hence more difficult to trace. Careful attention to grounding and shielding can minimize problems from this source.

Make sure that the environmental requirements of the hardware components are properly met. This might require building a separate enclosure for the DAC system to protect it from heat and dust.

11.6 SYSTEM DOCUMENTATION

The documentation of the DAC system should include the following items:

1. vendor-supplied documentation on all hardware and software
2. diagnostic programs and test results
3. a description of the DAC system consisting of the functional specifications, design specifications, system manual, user manual, system integration tests, and test results
4. documentation of hardware developed in-house consisting of functional specifications, design specifications, user manual, and system manual
5. documentation of software developed in-house consisting of functional specifications, design specifications, user manual, system manual, and source listings

User manuals should describe how the system is to be operated and should be written at the level of expertise of the operator. System manuals are meant for system maintenance people and should contain detailed description of the system structure and system components.

11.7 SYSTEM MAINTENANCE

Procedures for maintaining the system should be developed when the system is installed. This should include routine maintenance items such as

1. cleaning of disk heads
2. cleaning of electrical contacts
3. checking of battery used in power backup systems
4. backing up of programs and data in a protected location away from the site where DAC is located
5. downloading and uploading of programs and data from/to the mainframe computer
6. updating of system to reflect corrections and fixes announced by component manufacturers

Procedures should also be established to deal with system failure:

1. sequence of test programs to be run to isolate the cause of trouble
2. corrective actions to be taken in case of system failures
3. list of persons who are responsible for system maintenance
4. list of service representatives and spare parts suppliers

As with large computer systems, it is possible to enter into maintenance agreements with companies to protect against possible system failure. This will only apply to purchased components of the DAC system and will not be valid for the complete DAC system unless it was purchased as one unit from a single vendor.

During the first few months of operation, hardware is likely to be under warranty from the manufacturer. Hence try to run through all the system tests at this stage to detect any problems before the warranty period expires.

Software manufacturers frequently release updates to their product. This may merely involve correcting some bugs in the earlier version, or it may be an enhanced version of the product. Check to make sure that it is compatible with the rest of the system hardware and software before installation.

SUMMARY

In this chapter, we have tried to outline the step-by-step procedures for setting up a DAC system from scratch. Many of the procedures are similar to those followed in any engineering project. The key principles emphasized here are

Know what you want to do.

Try to accomplish your goals with a minimum of software and hardware development.

Document the system thoroughly.

Obviously, time, budget, and availability of trained personnel will all influence the final design. An understanding of the basic concepts discussed in this book will help you make decisions with confidence.

REFERENCES

HARRISON, J. J., ED. *Minicomputers in Industrial Control: An Introduction.* Research Triangle Park, NC: Instrument Society of America, 1978.
This book contains a number of chapters on justifying computer usage, planning and designing a system, implementing a system, and preparing system documentation. It is oriented mainly toward larger DAC projects, but many principles carry over to smaller systems as well.

APPENDIX A

Magazines
and Journals
in the Data Acquisition
and Control Area

The two magazines listed below are a good source of information regarding the use of microcomputers in DAC applications. They feature product reviews and book reviews. The articles are useful in learning about specific DAC applications.

> *Personal Engineering and Instrumentation News*
> 28 Rice St.
> Newton Center, MA 02159
> Phone (617) 969-7274

> *Intelligent Instruments and Computers*
> Applications in the Laboratory
> Lawler Communications Co.
> 154 East Boston Post Rd.
> Mamaroneck, NY 10543
> (914) 698-6655

The following two journals also feature articles related to applications of computers in the laboratory:

> *American Laboratory*
> International Scientific Communications, Inc.
> 808 Kings Hwy.
> Box 827
> Fairfield, CT 06430
> (203) 576-0500

Analytical Chemistry
American Chemical Society
1155 16th St., NW
Washington, DC 20036
(202) 872-8065

The following trade magazines address control and instrumentation issues in industrial applications:

Chilton's Instrumentation and Control Systems
Chilton Co.
Chilton Way
Radnor, PA 19089
(215) 964-4418

InTech: The International Journal of Instrumentation and Control
Instrument Society of America
67 Alexander Dr.
Box 12277
Research Triangle Park, NC 27709
(919) 549-8411

Control Engineering: For Designers of Control and Instrumentation Equipment and Systems Worldwide
1301 S. Grove Ave.
P.O. Box 1030
Barrington, IL 60010
(312) 381-1840

There are a large number of publications in the area of microcomputers. The following magazine is one of the oldest and carries a fair amount of information on all types of microcomputers:

Byte: The Small Systems Journal
McGraw-Hill, Inc.
70 Main St.
Peterborough, NH 03458
(603) 924-9281

There are magazines devoted to specific microcomputers. Owners of IBM PC and compatible computers will find the following magazine quite useful:

PC Magazine: The Independent Guide to IBM Computers
Ziff-Davis Publishing Co.
Computer Publications Division

One Park Ave.
New York, NY 10016
(212) 503-3500

Owners of the Macintosh family of computers can also find specific magazines related to this computer. See for example

Macworld: The Macintosh Magazine
   PCW Communications, Inc.
   501 Second St.
   San Francisco, CA 94107

There are also magazines devoted to software products. *Science Software Quarterly* is specifically oriented toward scientific software:

Science Software Quarterly
   Arizona State University
   Center for Environmental Studies
   Tempe, AZ 85287

Appendix B

Directory of Manufacturers

This appendix contains a partial listing of companies that market products for data acquisition and control using microcomputers. The list is by no means complete. For up-to-date information you are advised to consult current trade magazines. Two other directories that you might find useful are

Personal Engineering Manufacturers Directory
Published by Personal Engineering Communications
28 Rice St.
Newton Center, MA 02159
(617) 969-7274

Personal Engineering Resource Directory
Published by Lotus Development Corp.
55 Cambridge Parkway
Cambridge, MA 02142

Disclaimer. The author does not guarantee, recommend, or endorse any of the products listed here and elsewhere in this book. The reader should contact the vendor concerned for full details regarding the products listed. The author also does not make any warranties with respect to the accuracy and completeness of this directory. All information presented here and elsewhere in this book concerning specific companies and products is based on the author's best knowledge at the time this book was written.

ADDRESS LIST OF COMPANIES

Acrosystems Corp.	66 Cherry Hill Dr. P.O. Box 487 Beverly, MA 01915	(617) 927-8885
Action Instruments	8601 Aero Dr. San Diego, CA 92123	(619) 279-5726
Analog Devices	Two Technology Way P.O. Box 280 Norwood, MA 02062	(617) 329-4700
BBN Software Products Corp.	10 Fawcett St. Cambridge, MA 02238	(617) 491-8488
Burr-Brown Corp.	P.O. Box 11400 Tucson, AZ 85734	(602) 746-1111
Capital Equipment Corp.	10 Evergreen Ave. Burlington, MA 01803	(617) 273-1818
Centec Corp.	Centec Building 11260 Roger Bacon Dr. Reston, VA 22090	(702) 471-6300
Centaurus Software, Inc.	4425 Cass St. Suite A San Diego, CA 92109	(619) 270-4552
CET Research Group, Ltd.	P.O. Box 2029 Norman, OK 73070	(405) 360-5464
Connecticut Microcomputer	P.O. Box 786 Brookfield, CT 06804	(203) 354-9395 or 1-800-4CMC-USA
Controlsoft, Inc.	7568 Briarcliff Parkway Middleburg Heights, OH 44130	(216) 234-5759
Cyber Research, Inc.	5 Science Park Center P.O. Box 9565 New Haven, CT 06536	(203) 786-5151 or 1-800-341-2525
Cyborg Corp.	342 Western Avenue Boston, MA 02135	(617) 782-9820
Data Acquisition Systems	349 Congress St. Boston, MA 02210	(617) 423-7691 1-800-DAS-1990

Data General Corp.	4400 Computer Dr. Westboro, MA 01580	(617) 366-8911
Data Translation	100 Locke Drive Marlboro, MA 01752	(617) 481-3700
Digital Equipment Corp.	Laboratory Data Products One Iron Way Marlborough, MA 01752	(617) 481-9511
Dynamic Solutions Corp.	61 South Lake Ave. Suite 305 Pasadena, CA 91101	(818) 577-2643
Elexor	P.O. Box 246 Morris Plains, NJ 07950	(201) 299-1615
Equinox Data Corp.	150 Nickerson St. Suite 200 Seattle, WA 98109	(206) 281-7327
Gantt Systems, Inc.	495 Main St. Metuchen, NJ 08840	(201) 494-7452
Gerry Engineering Software	13310 West Red Coat Dr. Rockport, IL 60441	(312) 257-5950
GW Instruments	P.O. Box 2145 Cambridge, MA 02141	(617) 624-4096
Hamilton	6 Pearl Court Allendale, NJ 07401	(201) 327-1444
Heuristics, Inc.	9723A Folsom Blvd. Sacramento, CA 95827	(416) 369-6606
Hewlett-Packard	1501 Page Mill Rd. Palo Alto, CA 94304	(213) 970-7500
ICS Electronics Corp.	2185 Old Oakland Rd. San Jose, CA 95131	(408) 263-4844
Intel	3065 Bowers Ave. Santa Clara, CA 95051	(408) 246-7501
Interactive Microwave, Inc.	P.O. Box 139 State College, PA 16804	(814) 238-8294
Interactive Structures, Inc.	146 Montgomery Ave. Bala Cynwyd, PA 19004	(215) 667-1713
IO Tech	23400 Aurora Rd. Cleveland, OH 44146	(216) 439-4091
Keithly Data Acquisition and Control, Inc.	210 Lincoln St. Boston, MA 02111	1-800-552-1115

Laboratory Technologies, Inc.	328 Broadway Cambridge, MA 02137	(617) 497-1010
Loyola Controls, Inc.	1099 N. Batavia St. Orange, CA 92667	(714) 639-0526
Macmillan Software Co.	866 Third Ave. New York, NY 10022	(212) 702-3241 or 1-800-348-0033
Metrabyte Corp.	440 Myles Standish Blvd. Taunton, MA 02780	(617) 880-3000
Microway	P.O. Box 79 Kingston, MA 02364	(617) 746-7341
Motorola Semiconductor Products, Inc.	P.O. Box 20912 Phoenix, AZ 85036	(602) 244-7100
Mountain Computer, Inc..	360 El Pueblo Rd. Scotts Valley, CA 95066	(408) 438-6650 or 1-800-458-0300
National Instruments	12109 Technology Blvd. Austin, TX 78727	(512) 250-9119 1-800-531-5066
Omega Engineering, Inc.	One Omega Drive Box 4047 Stamford, CT 06907	(203) 359-1660
Qua Tech, Inc.	478 E. Exchange St. Akron, OH 44304	(216) 434-3154
Radian Corp.	8501 Mo-Pac Blvd. P.O. Box 9948 Austin, TX 78766	(512) 454-4797
Real-Time Devices, Inc.	1930 Park Forest Ave. P.O. Box 906 State College, PA 16804	(814) 234-8087
Rogers Labs	2727 S. Croddy Way Suite E Santa Ana, CA 92704	(714) 751-0442
The Scientific Press	540 University Ave. Palo Alto, CA 94301	(415) 322-5221
Scientific Solutions, Inc.	6225 Cochran Rd. Solon, OH 44139	(216) 349-4030
Small Business Computers of New England	4 Limbo Lane P.O. Box 397 Amherst, NH 03031	(603) 673-0228

Starbuck Data Co.	P.O. Box 24 Newton Lower Falls, MA 02162	(617) 237-7695
Strawberry Tree Computers	1010 W. Fremont Ave. Sunnyvale, CA 94087	(408) 736-3083
Taurus Computer Products, Inc.	340 Commercial St. Manchester, NH 03101	(603) 623-7505
Taylor Industrial Software	12204 106th Ave. Edmonton, Alberta Canada TSN 3Z1	(403) 482-7547
Unkel Software, Inc.	62 Bridge St. Lexington, MA 02173	(617) 861-0181

Appendix C

Decimal-to-Binary Conversion Chart

The following table can be used to obtain the 8-bit binary representation of decimal numbers in the range 0–255.

1	0 0 0 0 0 0 0 1	24	0 0 0 1 1 0 0 0
2	0 0 0 0 0 0 1 0	25	0 0 0 1 1 0 0 1
3	0 0 0 0 0 0 1 1	26	0 0 0 1 1 0 1 0
4	0 0 0 0 0 1 0 0	27	0 0 0 1 1 0 1 1
5	0 0 0 0 0 1 0 1	28	0 0 0 1 1 1 0 0
6	0 0 0 0 0 1 1 0	29	0 0 0 1 1 1 0 1
7	0 0 0 0 0 1 1 1	30	0 0 0 1 1 1 1 0
8	0 0 0 0 1 0 0 0	31	0 0 0 1 1 1 1 1
9	0 0 0 0 1 0 0 1	32	0 0 1 0 0 0 0 0
10	0 0 0 0 1 0 1 0	33	0 0 1 0 0 0 0 1
11	0 0 0 0 1 0 1 1	34	0 0 1 0 0 0 1 0
12	0 0 0 0 1 1 0 0	35	0 0 1 0 0 0 1 1
13	0 0 0 0 1 1 0 1	36	0 0 1 0 0 1 0 0
14	0 0 0 0 1 1 1 0	37	0 0 1 0 0 1 0 1
15	0 0 0 0 1 1 1 1	38	0 0 1 0 0 1 1 0
16	0 0 0 1 0 0 0 0	39	0 0 1 0 0 1 1 1
17	0 0 0 1 0 0 0 1	40	0 0 1 0 1 0 0 0
18	0 0 0 1 0 0 1 0	41	0 0 1 0 1 0 0 1
19	0 0 0 1 0 0 1 1	42	0 0 1 0 1 0 1 0
20	0 0 0 1 0 1 0 0	43	0 0 1 0 1 0 1 1
21	0 0 0 1 0 1 0 1	44	0 0 1 0 1 1 0 0
22	0 0 0 1 0 1 1 0	45	0 0 1 0 1 1 0 1
23	0 0 0 1 0 1 1 1	46	0 0 1 0 1 1 1 0

#										#									
47	0	0	1	0	1	1	1	1	1	95	0	1	0	1	1	1	1	1	1
48	0	0	1	1	0	0	0	0	0	96	0	1	1	0	0	0	0	0	0
49	0	0	1	1	0	0	0	0	1	97	0	1	1	0	0	0	0	0	1
50	0	0	1	1	0	0	0	1	0	98	0	1	1	0	0	0	0	1	0
51	0	0	1	1	0	0	0	1	1	99	0	1	1	0	0	0	0	1	1
52	0	0	1	1	0	1	1	0	0	100	0	1	1	0	0	1	1	0	0
53	0	0	1	1	0	1	1	0	1	101	0	1	1	0	0	1	1	0	1
54	0	0	1	1	0	1	1	1	0	102	0	1	1	0	0	1	1	1	0
55	0	0	1	1	0	1	1	1	1	103	0	1	1	0	0	1	1	1	1
56	0	0	1	1	1	0	0	0	0	104	0	1	1	0	1	0	0	0	0
57	0	0	1	1	1	0	0	0	1	105	0	1	1	0	1	0	0	0	1
58	0	0	1	1	1	0	0	1	0	106	0	1	1	0	1	0	0	1	0
59	0	0	1	1	1	0	0	1	1	107	0	1	1	0	1	0	0	1	1
60	0	0	1	1	1	1	1	0	0	108	0	1	1	0	1	1	1	0	0
61	0	0	1	1	1	1	1	0	1	109	0	1	1	0	1	1	1	0	1
62	0	0	1	1	1	1	1	1	0	110	0	1	1	0	1	1	1	1	0
63	0	0	1	1	1	1	1	1	1	111	0	1	1	0	1	1	1	1	1
64	0	1	0	0	0	0	0	0	0	112	0	1	1	1	0	0	0	0	0
65	0	1	0	0	0	0	0	0	1	113	0	1	1	1	0	0	0	0	1
66	0	1	0	0	0	0	0	1	0	114	0	1	1	1	0	0	0	1	0
67	0	1	0	0	0	0	0	1	1	115	0	1	1	1	0	0	0	1	1
68	0	1	0	0	0	1	1	0	0	116	0	1	1	1	0	1	1	0	0
69	0	1	0	0	0	1	1	0	1	117	0	1	1	1	0	1	1	0	1
70	0	1	0	0	0	1	1	1	0	118	0	1	1	1	0	1	1	1	0
71	0	1	0	0	0	1	1	1	1	119	0	1	1	1	0	1	1	1	1
72	0	1	0	0	1	0	0	0	0	120	0	1	1	1	1	0	0	0	0
73	0	1	0	0	1	0	0	0	1	121	0	1	1	1	1	0	0	0	1
74	0	1	0	0	1	0	0	1	0	122	0	1	1	1	1	0	0	1	0
75	0	1	0	0	1	0	0	1	1	123	0	1	1	1	1	0	0	1	1
76	0	1	0	0	1	1	1	0	0	124	0	1	1	1	1	1	1	0	0
77	0	1	0	0	1	1	1	0	1	125	0	1	1	1	1	1	1	0	1
78	0	1	0	0	1	1	1	1	0	126	0	1	1	1	1	1	1	1	0
79	0	1	0	0	1	1	1	1	1	127	0	1	1	1	1	1	1	1	1
80	0	1	0	1	0	0	0	0	0	128	1	0	0	0	0	0	0	0	0
81	0	1	0	1	0	0	0	0	1	129	1	0	0	0	0	0	0	0	1
82	0	1	0	1	0	0	0	1	0	130	1	0	0	0	0	0	0	1	0
83	0	1	0	1	0	0	0	1	1	131	1	0	0	0	0	0	0	1	1
84	0	1	0	1	0	1	1	0	0	132	1	0	0	0	0	1	1	0	0
85	0	1	0	1	0	1	1	0	1	133	1	0	0	0	0	1	1	0	1
86	0	1	0	1	0	1	1	1	0	134	1	0	0	0	0	1	1	1	0
87	0	1	0	1	0	1	1	1	1	135	1	0	0	0	0	1	1	1	1
88	0	1	0	1	1	0	0	0	0	136	1	0	0	0	1	0	0	0	0
89	0	1	0	1	1	0	0	0	1	137	1	0	0	0	1	0	0	0	1
90	0	1	0	1	1	0	0	1	0	138	1	0	0	0	1	0	0	1	0
91	0	1	0	1	1	0	0	1	1	139	1	0	0	0	1	0	0	1	1
92	0	1	0	1	1	1	1	0	0	140	1	0	0	0	1	1	1	0	0
93	0	1	0	1	1	1	1	0	1	141	1	0	0	0	1	1	1	0	1
94	0	1	0	1	1	1	1	1	0	142	1	0	0	0	1	1	1	1	0

143	1	0	0	0	1	1	1	1	1	191	1	0	1	1	1	1	1	1	1
144	1	0	0	1	0	0	0	0	0	192	1	1	0	0	0	0	0	0	0
145	1	0	0	1	0	0	0	0	1	193	1	1	0	0	0	0	0	0	1
146	1	0	0	1	0	0	0	1	0	194	1	1	0	0	0	0	0	1	0
147	1	0	0	1	0	0	0	1	1	195	1	1	0	0	0	0	0	1	1
148	1	0	0	1	0	1	1	0	0	196	1	1	0	0	0	1	1	0	0
149	1	0	0	1	0	1	1	0	1	197	1	1	0	0	0	1	1	0	1
150	1	0	0	1	0	1	1	1	0	198	1	1	0	0	0	1	1	1	0
151	1	0	0	1	0	1	1	1	1	199	1	1	0	0	0	1	1	1	1
152	1	0	0	1	1	0	0	0	0	200	1	1	0	0	1	0	0	0	0
153	1	0	0	1	1	0	0	0	1	201	1	1	0	0	1	0	0	0	1
154	1	0	0	1	1	0	0	1	0	202	1	1	0	0	1	0	0	1	0
155	1	0	0	1	1	0	0	1	1	203	1	1	0	0	1	0	0	1	1
156	1	0	0	1	1	1	1	0	0	204	1	1	0	0	1	1	1	0	0
157	1	0	0	1	1	1	1	0	1	205	1	1	0	0	1	1	1	0	1
158	1	0	0	1	1	1	1	1	0	206	1	1	0	0	1	1	1	1	0
159	1	0	0	1	1	1	1	1	1	207	1	1	0	0	1	1	1	1	1
160	1	0	1	0	0	0	0	0	0	208	1	1	0	1	0	0	0	0	0
161	1	0	1	0	0	0	0	0	1	209	1	1	0	1	0	0	0	0	1
162	1	0	1	0	0	0	0	1	0	210	1	1	0	1	0	0	0	1	0
163	1	0	1	0	0	0	0	1	1	211	1	1	0	1	0	0	0	1	1
164	1	0	1	0	0	1	1	0	0	212	1	1	0	1	0	1	1	0	0
165	1	0	1	0	0	1	1	0	1	213	1	1	0	1	0	1	1	0	1
166	1	0	1	0	0	1	1	1	0	214	1	1	0	1	0	1	1	1	0
167	1	0	1	0	0	1	1	1	1	215	1	1	0	1	0	1	1	1	1
168	1	0	1	0	1	0	0	0	0	216	1	1	0	1	1	0	0	0	0
169	1	0	1	0	1	0	0	0	1	217	1	1	0	1	1	0	0	0	1
170	1	0	1	0	1	0	0	1	0	218	1	1	0	1	1	0	0	1	0
171	1	0	1	0	1	0	0	1	1	219	1	1	0	1	1	0	0	1	1
172	1	0	1	0	1	1	1	0	0	220	1	1	0	1	1	1	1	0	0
173	1	0	1	0	1	1	1	0	1	221	1	1	0	1	1	1	1	0	1
174	1	0	1	0	1	1	1	1	0	222	1	1	0	1	1	1	1	1	0
175	1	0	1	0	1	1	1	1	1	223	1	1	0	1	1	1	1	1	1
176	1	0	1	1	0	0	0	0	0	224	1	1	1	0	0	0	0	0	0
177	1	0	1	1	0	0	0	0	1	225	1	1	1	0	0	0	0	0	1
178	1	0	1	1	0	0	0	1	0	226	1	1	1	0	0	0	0	1	0
179	1	0	1	1	0	0	0	1	1	227	1	1	1	0	0	0	0	1	1
180	1	0	1	1	0	1	1	0	0	228	1	1	1	0	0	1	1	0	0
181	1	0	1	1	0	1	1	0	1	229	1	1	1	0	0	1	1	0	1
182	1	0	1	1	0	1	1	1	0	230	1	1	1	0	0	1	1	1	0
183	1	0	1	1	0	1	1	1	1	231	1	1	1	0	0	1	1	1	1
184	1	0	1	1	1	0	0	0	0	232	1	1	1	0	1	0	0	0	0
185	1	0	1	1	1	0	0	0	1	233	1	1	1	0	1	0	0	0	1
186	1	0	1	1	1	0	0	1	0	234	1	1	1	0	1	0	0	1	0
187	1	0	1	1	1	0	0	1	1	235	1	1	1	0	1	0	0	1	1
188	1	0	1	1	1	1	1	0	0	236	1	1	1	0	1	1	1	0	0
189	1	0	1	1	1	1	1	0	1	237	1	1	1	0	1	1	1	0	1
190	1	0	1	1	1	1	1	1	0	238	1	1	1	0	1	1	1	1	0

239	1	1	1	0	1	1	1	1	1
240	1	1	1	1	0	0	0	0	0
241	1	1	1	1	0	0	0	0	1
242	1	1	1	1	0	0	0	1	0
243	1	1	1	1	0	0	0	1	1
244	1	1	1	1	0	1	1	0	0
245	1	1	1	1	0	1	1	0	1
246	1	1	1	1	0	1	1	1	0
247	1	1	1	1	0	1	1	1	1
248	1	1	1	1	1	0	0	0	0
249	1	1	1	1	1	0	0	0	1
250	1	1	1	1	1	0	0	1	0
251	1	1	1	1	1	0	0	1	1
252	1	1	1	1	1	1	1	0	0
253	1	1	1	1	1	1	1	0	1
254	1	1	1	1	1	1	1	1	0
255	1	1	1	1	1	1	1	1	1

Index